Jesus,
THE SON OF GOD,
Poetry

Kevin Millage

ISBN 978-1-64559-146-7 (Paperback)
ISBN 978-1-64559-147-4 (Hardcover)
ISBN 978-1-64559-148-1 (Digital)

Copyright © 2019 Kevin Millage
All rights reserved
First Edition

All rights reserved. No part of this publication may be reproduced, distributed, or transmitted in any form or by any means, including photocopying, recording, or other electronic or mechanical methods without the prior written permission of the publisher. For permission requests, solicit the publisher via the address below.

Covenant Books, Inc.
11661 Hwy 707
Murrells Inlet, SC 29576
www.covenantbooks.com

I Am Ready

Am I ready for Jesus!
White Horse Jesus will ride on
Down to this Earth in the clouds.
I shall watch and wait for Him.

I say, "May it be today!"
I know in my heart He'll come,
I hope I will be with Him,
Jesus, the one and only Son.

The signs of the times is God!
All Christians shall continue
To live victorious today.
We imitate the Lord Jesus.

God's holiness important!
Holy Father amazing
Jesus is for mankind now.
A sanctified holy life.

I am always listening!
His story is of my Lord.
He shall never forget me.
He told me to remember.

He is preparing heaven!
Heaven that Jesus promised.
On lands that Christians die,
It is my goal to be there.

God is over creation!
From now and forevermore,
I see what the Bible says.
Holy Spirit open up.

One day Jesus will judge life!
I hope He tells me well done.
My walk is with my Jesus.
This is the God I do know.

Life's Vapor

It needs to be told
A story of old
It is not too long.
It sings like a song.

Truth of a new life.
Jesus I do give
My time to Your Way
As I live each day.

A believer breathe
Carried to my death.
I strove to tell all
The lost by my call.

I chose not to sin,
For I do need Him.
Forgive my actions
Of my distractions.

A Bible ready
Makes my day steady.
I seek my own call
On my knees I fall.

God's wisdom I strove
To develop love
By the Scriptures
To be more sure.

I choose and retained
Holiness explained.
It is forever
To be delivered.

My maturity
Brings security.
I grew and I knew
My God stayed true.

The cost of the cross
Where God never loss,
For the devil knew
His days will be few.

Founder of my soul,
Jesus made me whole
Carried in His arms
When those wished me harm.

I praise and worship
Voicing His Lordship
Over my giving
In surrendering.

Father, I do sin
To take to the Son.
Holy Spirit moves
Me to God I love.

Advocate Jesus
Who truly knows us
Going to rule all
Answering His call.

My life's vapor
Going to Savior
Jesus as I say
I'm going to pray.

Jesus Forever

I am a dreamer
Who loves my Jesus.
He inspired me
To follow my God.

My time spent with
God makes life easier.
I read my Bible
To know God's own word.

People think they are
Above Jesus Christ
By the way they act,
Fall apart today.

Jesus is not a
Short-term fix today.
He moves my own life
Beyond my own faults.

I do remember
These wondering thoughts
From ideas I had,
Never satisfied.

There's more to Jesus.
I do gladly spend
Time in the scriptures.
There is happiness.

Life changes onward
To never stop now.
I am no doubter,
I am with Jesus.

Christian, it's final.
This daily living,
I obey Jesus,
Through situations.

A Parent's Actions

Teach children well
With encouragement.
Do be loving
Like Jesus is.

Parents need to
Give words of hope
To develop
Children's actions.

Teach your children
To continue
To pray onto
Holy Jesus.

In Sunday School,
Let them reach out
To Holy God.
Jesus loves them.

Your children see
Your own actions
By the way you
Follow Jesus.

Let your children
Feel security
And happiness;
God's guidance.

Have your children
To encourage
Friends to Sunday
School each week.

Children needs you
To be present
In their own lives
As they grow up.

A Sad Old Story

Heaven was your goal,
But the world won.
A sad old story
To once a Christian.

Earlier you walked
And talked with Jesus.
You said you loved Him.
Now you turn your back.

What happened to you?
Once you were on fire
Wanting to win all
To the Lord Jesus.

Was the goal too high?
Was the walk too hard?
Did you know your walk
Was to go to heaven?

Sinning enticed you.
You could not stop the
Running after world,
So you surrendered.

Satan finally
Got your eyes off God.
Now you go after
Whatever you want.

You said you could not
Help it due to the
Sin nature you have
Sinless life is gone.

Do remember God
Has given Jesus
To forgive your sins,
So come back to God.

Actions

Do call, God,
Out to me
With actions
As I pray.

I have, God,
My Bible
To go out
With God's Word.

Speak on, God,
To the lost
Before me
So hurting.

It's love, God,
They search for
In their own
Vices now.

My hope, God,
Shows only
You Jesus,
And not me.

You saved, God,
Them who asks
You into
Their own heart.

You do, God,
Send to hell
When lost do
Reject You.

You are, God,
Words of Life
Shown onto
Lost people.

Why do, God,
Some reject
When others
Do receive?

Then I, God,
Just go to
Explain to
The seekers.

Jesus, God,
Is the One
who answers
Their questions.

Tell them, God,
Life's questions
Are diverse
I'll look up.

Tired, God,
When the day is so long,
Work and church.

Need help, God,
Looking up
The Scripture
They ask for.

All to God I Do Believe

Judged guilty back then
When He had committed
Nothing worth crucifying.
All to God I do believe.

Father God requires it.
I gave my life to Jesus
Who hung on wooden cross.
All to God I do believe.

He died on wooden cross.
His body was taken
Down from the wooden cross.
All to God I do believe.

He was buried in the tomb.
All hope was gone by the
Disciples due to death.
All to God I do believe.

He is risen out of
The sealed and closed tomb,
It was closely guarded.
All to God I do believe.

Jesus ascends up
To the place He's making.
This makes me so happy.
All to God I do believe.

Now I wait for
His return from Heaven
He's making. He shall return as King.
All to God I do believe.

No to sin, yes to grace,
Forgiven and washed
By the blood of Jesus.
All to God I do believe.

Amen

I am thinking, Amen
My life is on Jesus.
Nobody can remove,
Especially Satan.

I do believe, Amen
My belief on Jesus.
Faithful servant today,
Especially to God.

I can trust God, Amen
My hope is on Jesus.
Forever Savior,
I believe what you say.

I will love God, Amen
My love is on Jesus.
Happiness for others,
Me is to be last place.

I'm forgiven, Amen
My new life on Jesus.
Continue towards people,
Show them I do care.

I do tell them, Amen
I witness on Jesus
Redemption is for me,
A new creation now.

I will pray on, Amen
I do talk to Jesus,
Patiently listening,
I will forever pray.

I will be true, Amen
My own actions, Jesus.
Teachable to act more
Wise using my Bible.

Antichrist

In this world
I am running,
"You need me now,"
Said with gusto.

Another day
Of being self,
"I am your man,"
Said in his speech.

Stick to my plans
We'll be OK.
"Like me always,"
Said his greatness.

No one can do
It but myself.
"I be so good,"
You'll be amazed.

Great things he'll do
With confidence.
"Look upon me,"
Said his ego.

My followers
Must know I speak,
"Like it or not,"
It'll be my way.

If it's his way
Watch out people.
"I do my thing,"
Said his image.

Belonging

Stay awake! I shall pray onward
Do not let the devil play too.
Keep in the scriptures, memorize,
For there will be a victory.

Take my hand! I shall be guided
There are snares and traps today.
I shall pray, praise, and love God.
It is Glory to my Lord Jesus.

Listen too! I heard from Jesus
Take it to the Lord who cares.
I do continue to obey
The God who has delivered me.

I do know! God is very good
My thoughts do stay close to God.
I gladly share to others Jesus.
I share the Holy Bible.

Forever! Heaven is my goal
My heart I give to my Jesus.
The Bible says there is a race.
It must be finished to the end.

Excellent! I have faith in God
Grace, I continue to live in.
My works are not the true way.
My heart loves my Lord Jesus.

Sharing God! This make me happy
Tell all who shall pass on by.
I go out to the open fields
Where many are lost without God.

Is it I! Take sin away now
This action I do need to do.
God wants life to be His only.
God does want my obedience.

Bye Sin That Clings On

No more willful sin.
Gone from my own life.
It had brought me down.
Bye sin that clings on.

Yes, I will be true.
I always want to.
Tell the people too.
Bye sin that clings on,

There is no maybe.
Saved I am now.
I have turned away.
Bye sin that clings on.

Today is new life.
Gave my heart to God.
Jesus is my Lord.
Bye sin that clings on.

Tomorrow, I live.
This is Lord willing.
I have been redeemed.
Bye sin that clings on.

Forever, I'll be.
God's child you'll know.
Sanctified I'll be.
Bye sin that clings on.

In life, do not lose.
This life is so short.
Saved, if sin, not saved.
Bye sin that clings on.

In death, I will live.
My soul be with God.
There is a heaven.
Bye sin that clings on.

Christian Believer

Believer receiver of our God's Grace
This is the only
Way to a Holy God.
There's no amount of money that can save you.
It is only our faith in Jesus Christ.

What kind of faith are we talking about?
It is saving faith in Jesus our Lord.
Let Jesus's blood wash you clean today
He died on Calvary to take our sins.

Never let Satan fool you about sins.
He wants you to work for your salvation.
Let the World he rules saturate you
Lukewarm Christians will not go to heaven.

Holy Spirit keep us on narrow way.
Wide is the path to everlasting hell.
Do read God's Word from the Holy Bible
This is the first belief in keeping on track.

Where would we be without changes in life?
Daily prayers and our actions are God's way.
We must earnestly do what Jesus says
This is obedience to be Christian.

Someday we will see Jesus in heaven.
This makes many happy thinking on this. If heaven is not your goal
 today too, what is keeping us here on planet Earth?

Creator Father of all of people,
Give us Jesus from our hearts to love.
When living here on this land we call home,
Christians treat all as brothers and sisters.

Do bless us Lord Jesus with a true race.
We hold back nothing on showing people.
It is all about reaching our today
The Gospel story from finish to end.

Christians

All I do want, God is to obey You.
Jesus is not just
A passing new fad.

Christians are dying
For their own beliefs.
Eroding freedom continue advance.

Times are getting bad.
Government telling
Christians to go against their beliefs.

If we do speak out,
The world makes fun
Of Christian views, especially TV.

We as true Christians pray
for our leaders
In the high places.
Jesus put them there.

Powerful tries to
Silence the Christians.
We are to love them
Who do use us.

Be kind to those who
Hate Christians too.
We are not to use
Any violence today.

Jesus said, "Those who
hate me will hate you."
Jesus knew we will
Be hated by the world.

Nowadays political
Correctness used by
Many to silence
The majority.

Do not cave into
The world's powers.
Faith in Jesus Christ
Is what we do need.

The Christian armor
Needs to be applied.
There are Christians
Running defeated.

Hold up the Bible
Stay true to the Trinity.
Father forgive us
When we do worry.

Satan has many
People in our land.
They belong to him.
They do go out too.

As time goes onward,
Those who are Christians
Will grow stronger
In their own faith.

Do stay Christian
When the times are bad.
Christ will soon return
To take Christians home.

Now is the time to receive the Lord
Jesus into your own heart,
A new creation.

Create in Me True Faith

Create in me true faith.
I shall not delay
To be with Jesus,
Faithfully Yours my God.

God's Truth surrounding me.
I shall forever
Search the Holy Bible,
Freedom to not sin on.

Thanks to Jesus I live.
I am seeking You
With my prayers, God.
Thankfully I am blessed.

Sometimes, I do wonder.
Jesus did hang on
The cross; He obeyed.
Father loves me this much.

I am centered on God.
Trinity is true
Never to be denied;
Holy Bible teaches.

Time shall continue too.
God always before
Beginning and end.
This Living Messiah.

I am following God.
Belief always keeps
Me worshipping Him
I shall hold on to God.

Holy Spirit lives on.
Jesus returning
To conquer Satan
God is always in me.

Give me wisdom always,
God's Holy Bible
Read every day
Faith in Jesus Christ

I accept Jesus's gift,
Grace that is so free
Due to holiness,
Forever before God.

Truth from the Holy Bible.
Christian wanting all
People to accept,
I will go to the lost.

They do reject God's Word.
They do prefer this
Worldwide system,
Satan's shall lose too.

I go to Jesus, God.
He hears me always
Without him sleeping,
Always a knocking.

Do live in me Jesus.
Sin is now removed,
Yet Satan hates this.
God's power's greater.

God moves me forward.
I will not turn back
Towards my own sins.
I am a Christian now.

Every chance I get,
I praise and thank God
I surrender to Him.
I shall serve my Jesus.

Crucified Jesus

The news on Jesus
Is the wooden cross.
We had put Him on it.
The true story goes on.

The sins people had
Put God on the cross.
It took on Him our sins.
Why would God do this?

The Romans' actions
Against Jesus Christ
Was then to beat Him
And put Him on Cross.

The crowds mocked Him.
"Come on down, Jesus."
"Send Your Angels, God."
Why do you wait so?

Silent was Jesus
To the people there.
Then Jesus forgave,
Then in time, He died.

The sky had darkened
The winds increased on
Tombstones, people raised.
People were amazed.

Off the cross Jesus
Was carried to tomb
By two believers,
Ceremonial burial.

Romans sealed the tomb.
Placement of the guards
Around the closed tomb.
Will people remember?

Do You Know

Do you know God's
Bible about His early life
Just to have our Jesus
Speak to us as written.

Do you know Christ was born?
This event had happened
Just Bible prophecies
Being fulfilled back then.

Do you know Jesus grew?
A fact He developed
Just gaining the knowledge
Taught by His own father.

Do you know He amazed?
Doctors in the temple
Just at the age of twelve
By the knowledge He holds.

Do you know at thirty
He read what Isaiah
Just said in the past
Fulfilling the verses?

Do you know Jesus was
Tempted by the devil
Just as Jesus quoted
The written Scriptures then?

Do you know authority
Jesus had on demons
Just by quoting Scriptures
Because Jesus is God?

Dreams and Visions

They could not stop the dream!
They could not stop the vision!
This present situation,
I looked to God for guidance.

It says the young have dreams
And the old have visions
In the Holy Bible.
This is the age we're in.

Jesus is truly my God.
He is whom I do obey
In all my own beliefs.
It's Jesus in my own heart.

Will others have their dreams
Or their visions about God?
Someday when they are young
Or someday when they are old.

God's people had their own times.
John saw a future in the
Revelations in the Bible
The Christians are living on.

Joseph did dream the future.
He saw his own father
And his brothers bowed down.
This truly did happen.

Peter's vision was present.
The gentile was allowed in.
The blanket did come down
With unclean animals on it.

Will visions and dreams be
Given to men and women.
According to Bible,
It already has begun.

Faithful to God

Father, life is easier
Since Jesus is the center
Of my own daily living.
I will always be faithful.

My Lord, I do not want to
Be the center anymore.
This is when life is running
Me, instead of You, Jesus.

Nobody is more important
Than the Lord of my life.
In myself, there is an ego
I do have to get rid of it.

Life is not always easy
To be wholly sanctified.
It takes much praying and
Obeying to seek God's will.

Maturing, I do read the Bible.
I want to get to know Jesus.
Nothing is more important to
Me than a personal relationship.

Holy Spirit is inside of me
By guiding and by obeying
Jesus every teaching He gave.
I surrender my life to Jesus.

I lay down my sins to Jesus
Jesus had washed my own soul.
Never will I sin onward by
Willfully disobeying my God.

Jesus did a work in myself
To where even I am amazed.
I see myself differently from
The way I used to be in this world.

Father God

He is the Maker of the human race,
Adam and Eve were made to fellowship
With Father God where no sin was.
They were forbidden to eat one fruit.

Satan deceived Eve to eat the forbidden fruit.
Eve gave Adam to eat the forbidden fruit.
This is why the human race now sins.
Mankind were thrown out of the garden.

God killed an animal and skinned it.
Clothed Adam and Eve with the skin.
Now mankind must go by blood.
God made sure mankind knew this.

Eve was punished by the bearing of kids.
Adam had to till the land to have any food.
Cain and Abel were born as first children.
God was present with them and saw all.

Cain presented God with a fruit sacrifice.
Abel presented God with a blood sacrifice.
Abel was accepted for it was God's way.
Cain's fruit sacrifice God was rejected.

Cain's wrath caused him to kill his brother.
God tossed out Cain away from his family.
With Cain's mark, God said no one kills.
If one kills Cain, they will get seven times more.

Cain did have a family after killing Abel.
They did no fellowshipping with Father.
Seth was born next to Adam and eve
His generation had followed after his father.

Holy God did have a way to man redeemed.
Mankind had a fallen state due to Garden.
God wanted people to come before Him
He sent His only Son who became man.

This second Adam was named Jesus.
Jesus was born by a virgin mother.
Virgin mother and the Holy Spirit
She had become pregnant by God.

Mary was the Mother and Jesus the son.
She is blessed before any other woman.
Jesus as a child amazed all people too.
He amazed the rabbis with His knowledge.

Jesus never sinned anytime in His life.
Jesus just had to do His Father's will.
Faithful was Jesus in all He did do.
Holy Father God was pleased with Jesus.

At thirty, Jesus's own ministry had begun.
He said Father and Jesus is the "I Am."
Jesus brought back people who had died.
He did so many miracles before all.

Jesus is God/man the Father had sent.
This is why mankind sins can be removed.
His ministry He talked about His death.
His disciples did not really understand.

Cross of Calvary Crucifixion was the price.
This Lamb of God bearing all the sins.
Jesus laid down His own life for us.
He took the shame upon the cross then.

He went to Hades for the keys then.
He had risen from the empty tomb.
Jesus ascended up into heaven, glory.
Forever accomplishing His ministry.

Shortly after this, Jesus sent the Holy Spirit.
Mankind who accepted Jesus as their
Lord and Savior will receive the Holy Spirit.
Jesus will not force Himself on you.

Go Onward, Christian

Been to the altar,
I gave my own life
To Jesus my Lord
And my Savior.

I was justified
That very same day.
God continued to
Work on my life.

He especially
Gave me His own
Love that day I decided
To follow Jesus.

Likewise, I am glad
To give Him my heart.
I learn more each day
On the Ways of God.

Brothers and sisters,
I do know I am
Happy to be in
The house of the Lord.

Fellowshipping is
To see areas I
Sometimes do lack in,
Such as in singing.

Yet I'm a part of
The church in many
Areas I worship
Holy loving God.

Sin is very bad.
Now I do seek
God's guidance on being
Wholly sanctified.

Justified then to
Go onwards toward
A holy lifestyle.
An example today.

No more willful sin
No more excuses.
God is showing me
To be His child.

Turn to God today
And ask Him to be
Ready to not sin.
I want God closer.

People, do not stand
For less than He wants.
He wants to give us
The second blessing.

I need to grow on
By being Christlike
So others will want
God as Savior.

Lost do watch Christians
I know it says to
Be perfect in Christ.
This means Christ is first.

I do pray to God
For Godly wisdom.
There is much choices
On God's path for me.

Look around Christian,
See all the people
Who know not Jesus
Spread the word of God.

God Comforts My Soul.

I do need Jesus
When I am lonely.
Jesus does move me.
God comforts my soul.

God shows me love.
I shall never stop.
Jesus is very good.
God comforts my soul.

I am sanctified.
I am made Holy,
Jesus controlled life.
God comforts my soul.

This Holy Bible I do show to all.
Jesus I can reach.
God comforts my soul.

Wisdom I do have
Never matches God's.
Jesus moves me on.
God comforts my soul.

I'm true to Father;
He does change me so.
Jesus is Truly God.
God comforts my soul.

I'll meet with others
As I show Gospel.
Jesus really cares.
God comforts my soul.

Many good people
Will go on to hell.
Jesus from my heart.
God comforts my soul.

God's Sanctification

More today God's way.
Why do many wait?
Sanctification is
For all the Christians.

Christians are today
Justified where the
Bible calls them babes.
They are born again.

Some people do not
Understand much of
The holiness movement,
The Second Blessing.

Eternal Security,
I believe it is
Wrong to teach also.
Why keep on sinning?

Do mature Christians
Read and study too?
The Holy Bible
Says what it does say.

Beware what it does
Says in the Bible
About the hate of
The religious rulers.

Do love your
Christians if you see errors
That are very small.
Love's not puffed up.

Brothers and sisters,
Jesus does believe
We're to be perfect.
Do stop your sinning.

Bible colleges
True to Jesus's past
Why are they turning
Into atheistic?

There are churches that
Lost the Holy Ghost.
They are liberals,
Especially.

Liberals that goes
And say they do not
Believe in all the
Doctrines Christian holds.

Jesus said a lot
In the parables.
The fields are white
For the harvest too.

When the Great White
Throne shall be present,
Will you be sorry
That you had sinned?

Confess if you sin.
Get right with Jesus.
Go to Jesus by
Choosing not to sin.

God's Company

I do lack the best wordings
On telling others my hopes
There is much I am learning
From all the thoughts I do have.

God's light is from the Bible
To move me in sinless life
This truth does speak to myself
Amongst holiness I seek.

My inspirations towards God
Are growing while together
God speaks with authority
Through His workings today.

Wisdom, it's given to me
Through my prayers to God
Reverently, I accept
The teachings of the Scriptures.

When I am persecuted,
I shall praise my Jesus Christ
I'll tell others who inflict hurt,
Jesus still loves them.

The Lord tells me I am His
With an everlasting love;
I surrender all to God
who never left me lonely.

My commitment forever
Centered on my Holy God
Holiness is what I want
My entire life Dear Jesus.

God, Your greatness is present
To a redeemed saved person
You had knocked on my door,
In which, I had opened wide.

The cross and resurrection are my words
I tell to all, Father,
You're my tomorrow
To where I need company.

His promises I hold on
Knowing what He says is truthful
This I do to speak about
His wonderful reminders.

Glory to my Dear Jesus
Whom does know my own thinking;
I thank you for my joy
Just being with You today.

The words of God are moving
With my praises and worship;
Songs are presenting the Lord
My soul-searching beliefs.

Heaven bound to Jesus now
Until I finally get there
I followed the narrow path
To my Savior of the world.

I'm in God's company to
Continue believing Him
Jesus continues to shine
With his plan I'm moving on.

God's light is from the Bible
To move me in sinless life
This truth does speak to myself
Amongst holiness I seek

Wisdom, it's given to me
Through my prayers to God
Reverently, I accept
The teaching of the Scriptures.

The Lord tells me I am His
With an everlasting Love;
I surrender all to God
Who never left me lonely.

God, your greatness is present
To a redeemed saved persons;
You had knocked on my door,
In which, I had opened wide

His promises I hold on
Knowing what he says is truth
This I do to speak about
His wonderful reminders.

The words of God are moving
With my praises and worship
Songs are presenting the Lord
My soul-searching beliefs.

God's Time

He had come to Israel.
Loved and hated was God.
A time in His life, Savior,
For told by the prophets of old.

His love had showed compassion.
People came to hear Him speak.
A time when God, teacher,
Came and taught His plan.

Good was Jesus's own ways.
He is a man whom Truth lays.
A time and place, Father,
Sent His Son Jesus to us.

Worshipping our Holy God.
Jesus obeyed and prayed.
A time of showing love, Savior,
Taking the sins upon Himself.

He suffered before His Father.
This Cross he was put on then.
A time of dying, God's Son,
What looked like an end to all.

He is risen; He is alive forever.
No tomb held Jesus my Lord.
A time that awed them, the Life,
Giving all mankind a true hope.

Thank you, Jesus, for faith in You.
Praise and thanks, we tell all.
A time in our lives, worshipping,
Knowing what God had done for us.

Having Jesus in my Soul

Having Jesus in my soul,
I am now a justified man.
I had given up all sinning,
So I can be with Christ Jesus.

Having now Jesus in my soul,
I am now a sanctified man.
I am now filled with the Spirit
To live holy life before God.

Having now Jesus in my soul,
I know Satan has no grasp on me,
For Jesus now holds me only
To live my life to please Jesus.

Having now Jesus in my soul,
My life is all about my Lord.
My devotions are to serve God
By studying the Holy Bible.

Having now Jesus in my soul,
I'll go wherever God does say.
They do need Jesus in their lives
They are going to a place, hell.

Having now Jesus in my soul,
I decided no more turning back,
For I'm going to run the race
To the finish line of my life.

Having now Jesus in my soul,
I do accept the Grace of God.
The blood had washed me totally.
I am only going to God.

Having now Jesus in my soul,
I am shining my light to all
People who'll come into my life.
A witness whom will obey God.

He Drifted Away

He drifted to the World,
Falling downward Christian.
He finds relationships
More towards non-Christians.

Yes, he does feel ok.
He still thinks He is good.
He knows God's goodness
Is it on His own terms?

Life moves Him many ways.
He knows a Holy God,
At least no punishment.
Only love in his own life.

He does not talk to God.
Not like he used to talk.
Didn't He hide some Scripture,
Yet He is a quiet man.

Why does troubles do come?
He tells God I need help.
Two days has gone on by,
He does forget to thank.

Bitterness against God
If life left him behind.
His relationship did
Not survive in the end.

His own prays long ago
Slowly dwindled to rare.
He does not repent sin
Since he hardened his heart.

The Christians do have joy
How can he get some too?
In another decade,
He is totally lost.

Hello

Hello my Father;
I do acknowledge
His mighty power,
He had loved me so.

Hello to the Son
I do acknowledge
His true position,
Seeing the Man/God.

Hello Comforter
I do acknowledge
Holy Spirit too
Living within me.

Hello Trinity
I do acknowledge
There's only One God,
Forever living.

Hello Calvary
I do acknowledge
He'd died for me too,
Cruel Roman sentence.

Hello Salvation
I do acknowledge
Jesus as the Way,
Father I love You.

Hello He's Risen
I do acknowledge
Tomb did not hold Him,
Sealed by Pilate.

Hello to Heaven
I do acknowledge
The race before me,
Forward to the end.

Holiness

Jesus lives, Holiness.
I worship Father God
As the Holy Spirit
Continues to guide me.

I forever go on
With my love for Jesus.
He loves me and molds me
As a New Creature too.

The awesomeness of God
Who went to Calvary.
The Father allowed the
Son to be nailed to Cross.

I am truly amazed
By God's plan for mankind.
On this path Father gave,
Jesus was Resurrected.

Salvation is through the
Beloved Jesus Christ.
Jesus had freed us from
This horrible bondage.

I surrender to God
As a growing Christian.
Christianity moves
Me only to Jesus.

I shall make it, Jesus.
The path is so narrow
Without any detours.
No turning away now.

My desire is God
Where I am heaven bound.
Jesus is only way
That I'm going to live.

Humanity's Man

Unsaved due to pride
The cost was too high.
God, do you expect
Me to stop sinning?

Understand today,
I need my freedom.
No surrender to God.
Radical, I am.

People do like me,
So nice as I am.
My life is moving
To please mankind.

This world needs me.
People need to hear.
I speak my own mind
Today I stand tall.

Do people seek me?
I truly am good,
Respectable.
Yes, I do stand out.

I felt like knowing;
I will go farther
In my intelligence.
I shall write a book.

Found I am aging
Since time never stops.
I did prove myself
To humanity.

I know, follow me.
I set people free.
I do as I please
Because I do know.

I Get It

God's Creation He said, "It's good."
It was done in seven days
These are twenty-four-hour days.
My God is mighty and able.

God made mankind in His image.
Almighty God made Adam first,
Yet Adam had no companion
God took Adam's rib and made Eve.

Noah built an Ark due to God's
Worldwide flood covering lands.
Only Noah's family were spared,
Along with animals in the Ark.

Moses had parted the Red Sea
Destroying Egypt's Army then.
He took the people to God's land.
This is Canaan Israel shall dwell.

Goliath challenged the Israelites
By boasting Our God is weaker.
Young David had killed Goliath
Using a slingshot in God's plan.

Elijah challenged wickedness
Of Ahab and Jezebel prophets;
God's fire licked up the sacrifice.
Jezebel prophets were then killed.

Jonah was swallowed by the big fish
He went the wrong way on Sea.
Spewing Jonah at Nineveh
Out of the belly of big fish.

Jesus was born in Bethlehem
According to the prophecies.
Mary was named in the Bible
Of the Virgin birth of Jesus.

Jesus's first miracle was wine
Made from ordinary water first.
There was a wedding in Cana
Where the couple ran out of wine.

The feeding of the five thousand
With only a little food then.
They sat in rows distributing food
Food left was put in baskets.

Jesus walked on the water
To where the apostles feared
The boat would sink very soon
Jesus calmed the sea in the end.

People came all around the land
To be healed by the Master's and.
He told people after healing
To sin no more from this day on.

Jesus died by Crucifixion;
Jesus risen three days after death. God had ascended to heaven
All prophecy completed by Jesus.

Jesus returns on a white horse
To defeat Satan's dominion.
This does speak the wicked also
Will end in the Lake of Fire.

I

I live in the dark.
I stay in the world.
I like life my way
I grasp it right now.

I dare this old God.
I swear to be me.
I learn to fight on
I sing it is mine.

I want to be fed.
I spend it on me.
I get what I want
I hold up my hands.

I found the right mix.
I turn to much sex.
I felt it is right
I swore I shall have.

I will make it right.
I now solve a lot.
I do not bow down
I lift up this life.

I do see the weak.
I am to be strong.
I took the wide road
I work to be me.

I do play with death.
I had a new plan.
I shall bend the rules
I got to have fun.

I drink with my friends.
I cuss when I want.
I fall to no one
I am true to none.

Inspiration

It's all due to Jesus in
God's Holy Bible.
The God I do follow
Is the Holy Trinity.

Only in Lord Jesus is
Whom I am inspired in.
I could do no writing
If Jesus was not God.

God is made up as
the Father, the Son,
And the Holy Spirit.
I got to know God.

My Father is inspiring
Coming to all mankind.
Without Jesus, I'm lost
To be hopelessly in sin.

I tried writing secular
Poetry a while back.
I felt I was very empty.
I was running from God.

It was in mankind's way
Of trying to please people.
People needed the Truth
People needed Jesus Christ.

Today my goals are to
Please only Jesus Christ.
My own soul does hunger;
The Word of God does move.

Jesus is knocking onward
For all to come to Him.
Poetry is part of my own
Expressions towards God.

It Is All Action

I obey God by reading the Bible.
This does keep me going to Jesus Christ,
For Jesus is the True Way to Father.
Holy Spirit always moves my own soul.

People! This is God's Way for me to go.
Trinity is present in the Bible.
Written by God's holy prophets today.
This is now the time to follow Jesus.

This Jesus is worshipped by my love,
And I am a Christian by my free choice.
I believe in the Holy Scriptures too.
No errors are present in the Bible.

It's God's grace I do hold on to only.
Works will not be the only way today.
This is God's own plan where we get it free.
Works will follow our actions to Jesus.

Pride does never satisfy forever.
What do I believe in my inner self?
I surrender my pride to Jesus
Remove this puffed-up attitude I have.

The true deal is only in Jesus Christ, died, buried, and resurrected
 in life.
Holy Spirit does move my soul today
To go to Jesus to get to Father.

I shall go on fishing for lost souls.
They are ever on my own mind today.
I do want to give the answers to life.
The right way to a Holy and Just God.

Some people believe their sins are too great,
Yet God is greater by forgiving sins.
Jesus, my Savior, came down to be man.
God's Son whom stayed to save all who'll come.

My God's Word is faithful to hold on to
My trust comes by knowing Jesus today.
Jesus had to stay within my own heart.
A love that shall show others there is hope

Jesus Gives

Faith, Jesus gives,
Does stay within me.
It grows like a
Mustard seed now.

Grace, Jesus gives,
Does stay within me.
Salvation is not Jesus is
By working for it.

Holy, Jesus gives,
Does stay within me.
Sanctified wholly
I am living now.

Blood, Jesus gives,
Does stay within me.
It removes my sins
To sin no more.

Love, Jesus gives,
Does stay within me.
God owns my soul.
I do love Him.

Strength, Jesus gives,
Does stay within me.
Powerful courage
To witness now.

Good, Jesus gives,
Does stay within me.
Just to be with
Jesus as I pray.

Just, Jesus gives,
Does stay within me.
Everything God
Does is His Will.

Life, Jesus gives,
Does stay within me.
I want to be
With my Jesus.

Truth, Jesus gives,
Does stay within me.
God/Man
Given by Father God.

Way, Jesus gives,
Does stay within me.
God shows salvation
In Jesus only.

Light, Jesus gives,
Does stay within me.
There is shining
In me Jesus.

Care, Jesus gives,
Does stay within me.
Jesus has the
Answers for me.

Help, Jesus gives,
Does stay within me.
God longs to be
There in all times.

Sword, Jesus gives,
Does stay within me.
The Holy Bible
Is used each day.

Peace, Jesus gives,
Does stay within me.
I feel His presence,
And it calms me.

Jesus Let Me Pray On

Jesus let me pray on
Do this poem made sense?
Can others understand?
Did I use the right words?

Use me God today
God's talents and God's gifts.
Please move all people
To what they need now.

Forgiven by Jesus,
Even when I'd failed.
The pieces were picked
Up and made whole too.

Sin's grieves my God.
My body does hate
Due to its effects.
A ruined witness.

I am sanctified
With Second Blessing.
I will sin no more
Willful disobeyed.

My life is with God.
It is God's control
And not my control
On Father's own throne.

Jesus does quote on
The Holy Bible.
The devil learned this
In the wilderness.

I do obey God,
And I shall submit
To Jesus my Lord.
This is forever.

My desires to sin
Like I did in past
God's blood washed away.
Satan has no hold.

Jesus redeemed me
My forever God.
Jesus had changed me
My light shall shine on.

I study God's Word.
Peace floods my soul.
I know life is short,
And I am older.

The Holy Bible
Talks about a life
Being very short
I'm an example.

Faith with Jesus Grace
Sends us to Jesus
Faith without His grace
Sends people to hell.

Salvation message
Christians do give out
To them where many
Don't know they do sin.

Jesus's peace is real.
Mankind's looking for
Anything that brings
Peace to their own soul.

People are so lost
When Jesus so near.
People travels to
A place of no hope.

My Brothers and Sisters

I'm going to have this hope
For my brothers and sisters.
Jesus is inspiration,
And I'm joyfully singing.

I'm going to have to give
For my brothers and sisters.
Jesus saves sinners today
On them who have given their hearts.

I'm going to give my love
For my brothers and sisters.
Jesus is love undeniable,
For He's true to his people.

I'm going to lift up God
For my brothers and sisters.
Jesus is above all gods,
Past, now, and future events.

I'm going to tell the truth
For my brothers and sisters.
Jesus knows all about us,
And He gave us the Bible.

I'm going to hold strong now
For my brothers and sisters
Jesus wants especially now
To bring His faith to others.

I'm going to be peaceful
For my brothers and sisters.
Jesus is the one to give
Peace to all the restless souls.

I'm going to have faith now
For my brothers and sisters.
Jesus is my own reason
To find His own example.

My Heart

My heart loves God
Of my own soul
He is my love,
And He shows love.

My heart chose God
The Creator
He is Father,
And He exist.

My heart goes to
Lord Jesus Christ
He is so Good,
And He is God.

My heart goes to
Holy Spirit
He is in me,
And He moves me.

My heart tells me
To worship God
He is Worthy,
And He draws me.

My heart grasps Truth
Jesus does give
He is Wisdom,
And He knows all.

My heart follows
The only Way
He is my guide,
And He leads me.

My heart shall stay
True to Jesus,
He is stable,
And He stays true.

Never Saved

If I am going to be happy,
It has to be on my terms.
I do want Jesus sometimes,
As long as He accepts me.

I have a Holy Bible also
This does keeps me on good terms.
I do take a verse to read
What I do believe it tells me.

I do give testimonies how
I was so blessed on my needs.
I do not want others to think
Less of my being different.

I'd strived to sound very good.
Especially to all my friends.
There are some radicals in church.
I'm always talking about them.

I do have a relaxed attitude.
I do not want to rock the boat.
God is a God that loves me.
I know He'll give me what I want.

I am holy because I was
Baptized as a baby at birth.
This will save my soul I know.
What else can God want today?

I do get answers from Jesus
Because I am so sincere.
I give God the best of me
All the time I'm around people.

If life does get harder now,
It is the devil doing it.
God will not let me suffer too.
He is Jesus who knows me.

No Time to Stop Our Race

No time to stop our race.
It is to God we love
To reach our goal today,
Endurance to the end.

Another day to go onward.
There is no turning back.
The world is calling us,
But too much heartache there.

What was our reason, Jesus?
We did need Love from God.
Our body has a soul,
It will live forever.

We shall live forever;
Let our search end with God.
The Christian life shall take
Us before Jesus's throne.

Why do Christians witness?
We know there is Jesus.
Our Father sent Jesus
To save us from our sins.

Onward! Do not go back
To go nowhere but pain.
Christians do have pain too.
Jesus will never leave.

Some say we have a crutch.
No, Jesus is the yoke
We put all burdens on.
He will show us he cares.

This theme is part of us.
We want all family
Members to be saved too
For each generation.

No God in Life

No God in life!
How will we live?
How will we die?
Hell is for them.

No God in life!
Love is Jesus
Love is our God.
Hell has no love.

No God in life!
Peace has left us.
Peace has just gone.
Hell has no peace.

No God in life!
Worms do live there
Worms do not die.
Hell has live ones.

No God in life!
Pain will keep us
Pain will grip us.
Hell shows hope gone.

No God in life!
Light of God gone
Light turns to dark.
Hell is so dark.

No God in life!
Pride did come too
Pride did move me.
Hell does not care.

No God in life!
Hate does go on.
Hate is shown too.
Hell's full of it.

No God in life!
Fear moves us so
Fear of what's there.
Hell will keep lost.

No God in Life!
Greed in our work
Greed in our play.
Hell is with us.

No God in life!
Price is too high
Price may go down.
Hell is for sure.

No God in life!
Rich can make it
Rich can live it.
Hell's full of rich.

No God in life!
Swear at our God
Swear with our mouths.
Hell is your place.

No God in life!
There goes our friends
There goes our thoughts.
Hell shall reach out.

No God in life!
Where will we start?
Where will we end?
Hell is so real.

No God in life!
Can I be good?
Can I be bad?
Hell is a place.

Obeying God

Jesus cares about
The way I do live
My example is
According to Bible.

My own prayer is
To be a child of God.
All I have I do is
Give to my Jesus.

With good attitude,
I do obey God.
Holiness people
Are consecrated.

Guidance in my life
Comes to me today
By Jesus my Lord.
I follow Jesus.

I do love Jesus.
He keeps me moving
With faith and grace.
Praise You and Thank You.

My future is His
I learned from the past.
Wisdom from
Jesus is my hope today.

I was delivered
From my wicked past.
Jesus, God had formed
Me as a Christian.

I know God saved me.
God's grace is all I
Do need for it's free.
No more to sinning.

On This Rock

On this Rock, I do see
I shall not hate people
Who do me wrong today.
I do read my Bible.

On this Rock, I know
Jesus is above me.
This Holy Living God
Is open to my soul.

On this Rock, I shall pray.
I shall obey His Ways
As my time moves onward.
Jesus stays the same too.

On this Rock, I do find
Peace that satisfies me.
His wisdom is to be
For me to be Christlike.

On this Rock, I'll obey
By my obedience.
I do give up all sins
To be pure to my God.

On this Rock, I need Him
Who does comfort my soul.
Teach me to be a man
Whom will not fail Jesus.

On this Rock, I see God's
Scriptures coming alive.
It tells me I do need
To be pondering it.

On this Rock, I want Him.
Father, I go before You
By going through Jesus.
Holy Spirit moves me.

On this Rock, I know time
Cannot change my Savior.
The Cross Jesus hanged
Took all my transgressions.

On this Rock, I shall stay
By not falling away.
Forgive me if I do
Happen to fail Jesus.

On this Rock, I have God's
Grace in my present life.
Faith is in Lord Jesus.
A gift I did receive.

On this Rock, I will stop
This wicked ugly sin.
I will live a true life
Where I choose not to sin.

On this Rock, I believe
In Holy Bible Truths.
This error-free Bible
Is God's Holy Scripture.

On this Rock, I am loved
Even when I failed God.
I know my Redeemer.
Myself needs true changing.

On this Rock, I will go
To my heavenly home.
My death is not the end
It is the beginning.

On this Rock, I have run
As a Christian should run,
And loved as a person.
I am a true Christian.

Our Lives

Jesus, my faith in God,
Makes me to kneel in love.
I shall give Him myself,
For this is how I feel.

Past a good deed along;
Make a person happy.
They need to hear Jesus,
Reading Holy Bible.

Tell the children today,
Jesus, do go to Him.
He will never leave you,
For Jesus cares a lot.

Teenagers, you need God
Live for Jesus today.
Plans were made long in past,
Christ died at Calvary.

Adults, give God your time
Do not be so busy.
Meet with Jesus, people
And worship Him in awe.

Elderly, keep on going;
To finish line so close.
Jesus shall give you hope
In beautiful heaven.

Keep your faith all people
Who has Jesus who stays.
Turn not away from God
When the times get harder.

Someday in Heaven Land,
We'll be in God's presence.
A new body we'll have
Going as the new bride.

Present Love

During my lifetime,
Jesus knows me best.
I continue on
Worshipping Jesus.

I do see God's true
Loving ways also.
It thrills me being
Surrendered, Jesus.

A calmness does come
Within my own life.
Jesus's true presence
Does strengthen myself.

I want more of
God's loving tenderness.
It starts within me
To love Jesus Christ.

Jesus is just like
Holy Bible says.
I want to know God
As I read His Word.

I'll never give up
While I am aging.
I continue on
Learning about God.

Gentle Spirit moves
Through my own body,
For Jesus showed me
The depth of His Love.

I say I do feel
The Holy Spirit.
He shows me a love
That never does fail.

Respectability Now

Do you get and deserve me?
Respectability now I
I'm mindful of my own pride.
My ego has shown just me.

Do I need fame's light this day?
Respectability now!
A billboard with my own face.
Glory to myself always.

Do I sin as I do laugh?
Respectability now!
I drove my personality.
My own life is to look on.

Do people wish to be me?
Respectability now!
They see my example too.
A person who has a life.

Do my dreaming brings you hope?
Respectability now!
I do not want to be old.
Nobody can stop my dreaming.

Do teach people about me?
Respectability now!
This is where I am going.
Just watch me amaze people.

Do be honor knowing me?
Respectability now!
Find out the way I fight on.
I do live in this world.

Do ask how I move people?
Respectability now!
I show them my own journey.
I went my way to be me.

Rise Up and Praise Him

Rise up and praise Him.
Tell God you worship Him.
The Son is worthy, God.
Jesus, I will pray to.

Rise up and praise Him.
Holy Spirit does move
My soul to follow Him.
Glory to Jesus Christ.

Rise up and praise Him.
I'll follow God with awe
At the power He has.
My King and my Lord God.

Rise up and praise Him.
Watch for Jesus's return.
He is coming some day
When the trumpet shall sound.

Rise up and praise Him.
The Word of God moves me.
Holy Bible shows me
The true sinless Jesus.

Rise up and praise Him.
Father I thank always
For sending to us Jesus,
The Alpha and Omega.

Rise up and praise Him.
I am forgiven now
Due to Jesus's actions,
The Cross of Calvary.

Rise up and praise Him.
I am a New Creature.
A follower of God,
Surrender to Jesus.

Rise up and praise Him.
I obey Holy God.
Holiness God requires
Of all of His children.

Rise up and praise Him.
God takes us to heaven
When the saved Christians
Are to be glorified.

Rise up and praise Him.
God rules all His people.
In His Hands, God molds us.
He sanctifies us in life.

Rise up and praise Him.
Receive a person saved
From his transgressions
As a babe in Christ.

Rise up and praise Him.
Show us and teach all
Christians, especially young.
Disciple them today.

Rise up and praise Him.
Seek out the lost people
To give their hearts to God.
Testify to the lost.

Satan Loses

What is Satan's lie?
It's no-winning cause.
Christians knows the Bible
Say Satan will lose.

Satan's deception
God does not deceive.
Deception comes from
Satan's hellish ways.

Jesus or Satan
Go up or go down.
Let heaven be yours.
Why go down to hell?

Are you a winner?
Are you a loser?
How do you know God?
Choice between the two.

Lake of Fire is true.
A separation.
No Holy God there
Only much anguish.

This day is not done!
You can have Jesus.
Realize in your life
Jesus can save you.

You say friends are there.
In hell, all alone
Without any friends
Comforting your pain.

Do know, Jesus saves.
Satan will be in
The Lake of Fire too.
This is his future.

Searching

I drop to my knees
I tried to be true.
No one cares to know
My life is failing.

I lived for myself
Yet I knew not why.
I did not want truth
I am not ready.

I do live in dread
Others sees myself.
Image of myself
Is so very wrong.

I did move onward
Without any hope.
I spent my money
On my own image.

I am serious
By working harder.
Life can be cruel
On the way upward.

I had to stop this.
I looked so inward.
Is there a real God?
Maybe, I will see.

My dusty Bible
I will try a church.
Shall the people see
How well I am dressed.

Church may become true
I may stay the same.
God may be the way.
I am a seeker.

Sending My Prayers

I am sending my prayers
To our foreign ministries.
My God who keeps moving
To the lost who came to Jesus.

I am sending my prayers
To our home ministries.
My God who keeps moving
To the lost who came to Jesus.

I am sending my prayers
To my pastor's ministries.
My God who keeps moving
To the lost who came to Jesus.

I am sending my prayers
To my father's examples.
My God who keeps moving
To the lost who came to Jesus.

I am sending my prayers
To my mother's examples.
My God who keeps moving
To the lost who came to Jesus.

I am sending my prayers
To all people's own burdens.
My God who keeps moving
To the lost who came to Jesus.

I am sending my prayers
To people everywhere.
My God who keeps moving
To the lost who came to Jesus.

I am sending my prayers
To people by witnessing.
My God whom keeps moving
To the lost who came to Jesus.

Show the Lost

Christians are to love all,
Especially God's own.
This is how all may know
The acts of true Christians.

Christians in our churches,
Let us get together
In our own fellowships
All across our own land.

We are all part of God's
Family with our gifts.
We worship with Christians
And with non-Christians.

We do want to show them,
The lost souls to come in
The church family now.
God will do the molding.

It is to fellowship
And to worship our God.
It is always to have
Our faith in God's Grace.

When problems do come up,
Go to God by praying.
Seek for wisdom so we
May know how to answer it.

Lost do need Jesus Christ
To save their own souls from
A fiery hot hell.
Show them it is their choice.

Persecution comes in
Many ways around world.
Let's cling close to Jesus
In all life's situations.

Something Missing

If God is not in you,
You are a true heathen.
A heathen knows not of God
They live more for this world.

You want it to go smoothly
As long as no work comes.
What is important "it"?
The search keeps on going.

Sleep each morning to
The sound of alarm bell.
It does not get better.
Can I snooze five also?

Traffic does come and goes.
Will I be late for work?
Work if you can call it,
Yet I will hang in there.

Pass the time away now
As the day goes onward.
Is there something missing?
Life really is not fair.

Lunch out or in today.
This choice is just way
Too demanding I see.
I now have to decide.

Routine need to change too.
What book can I now read?
It shall improve myself.
Always, I feel empty.

What you need is Jesus?
Your empty days be gone.
Be forgiven of your sins.
Start living for Jesus.

Stand with God

I do not know what is coming
In a world filled with violence.
This I do know there is One who
Will be there when I need His Hands.

Jesus continues to be a steady hand
As the times in my life does change.
I can depend on Him to live my life
With an ever presence with God.

Father knew me before I had come.
A choice I decided to give my life
Over to the ways of Holy God back then.
Father, Your Son died for me and you.

Holy Spirit uses His power to move
Me towards Crucified Jesus now.
He stands with the Holy Bible directing
Me to understanding just what it says.

I am open to hear a Word from God
In a place I found peace and quiet.
Get away from these noises that distract
In this world in such a fast hurry.

I do stand with God whom loves me
To obey Him always and not sin on.
When I do sin I ask for forgiveness
To the Holy Father through Jesus Christ.

God's ways are my ways from now on
Holy Bible teaches me about Holy God.
A Christian whom knows whom he believes
In with a desire to interpreting rightly.

Times moves on and on every day
Never to stop and see my own future.
This future I do leave with my Savior.
The present was decided in loving Him.

There is a way that is destruction.
A falling away that leads to the wide road.
It is inviting, yet is so very damnable.
Satan rules to fight the Christian today.

When my family moves away from God
My prayers to God is to save them.
Do not let my Christlikeness not be seen.
I know my example is sometimes imperfect.

Testify to my family whenever I can.
There is a peace with God's guidance.
I know what lays ahead for them
If they do not change their ways now.

I pray to God with a love for all people.
They are the ones who seem so far away.
Without anyone to tell them about God.
Missionaries I do support as much as I can.

Sometimes I wonder what life would be
If I grew up to accept God earlier.
I was sinful in my life before Jesus.
I wish I accepted Jesus's invitation then.

The invitation did come, and I accepted it.
My best decision I wanted Holy God.
Now I cannot imagine leaving God
For a cruel Satan who hates me.

What is this poem trying to get at?
God says in many ways He is the Way.
Will you stand with God and be His
Child forever when we are living?

I Will Do as I Please Too

Stubbornness is in my blood
Because I want it my way.
I will do as I please too.
This meanness comes easily.

Silliness is in my blood
Says the boys and the girls.
I will do as I please too.
This kid is wild and loud.

Wilderness surrounding me
As the eagle flies on.
I will do as I please too.
This life is to be myself.

Tiredness does come to me
For I played very hard now.
I will do as I please too.
I do want lots of laughter.

Wildness does keep me going
Without an end to pleasure.
I will do as I please too.
My ways keep me acting up.

Worthiness is to be me
Since I am the champion.
I will do as I please too.
A high-headed kid in clouds.

Naughtiness is to be stopped
As I want it orderly.
I will do as I please too.
Punished to their own bedroom.

Wickedness desires me
Says the kid's body language.
I will do as I please too.
Rebel, I belong to you.

Quietness is not to be found
Around homes I do reside.
I will do as I please too.
We do move very often.

Goriness when I do watch
Many television shows.
I will do as I please too.
My monster movies galore.

Carelessness in my actions
By doing it my own way.
I will do as I please too.
I really do know better.

Holiness is what you need
Yet this is not what you want.
I will do as I please too.
Someday when I get older.

Tardiness every day
To go and do your own chores.
I will do as I please too.
I am for getting a raise.

Churchliness in family
Makes me go to the service.
I will do as I please too.
Wake me up when church is done.

Tell me, Lord

My own way, I'm lost,
Understood nothing.
True, issues surfaced.
My grasp is not there.

Nothing had remained
Solid Holy God.
Jesus was a name
In Holy Bible.

Then I met Jesus,
Christian faith from God.
Stability found.
My search is over.

I ended my ways.
I accept God's Truth.
I shall always be
Listening closely.

Willful sin, no more.
There are gray areas.
Yet I shall pray on.
I do seek God's Will.

I'll love You always;
I'll obey my God.
You are with me here.
I'm listening, God.

Every Word too.
Holy Bible is
My own desire
To say thank you God.

I'll tell others God
About Salvation
Only through Jesus
Unto the Father.

The Dart Is in Me

I go to sleep now.
God will delay His
Coming back today.
The dart is in me.

World kept me too.
Christian backsliding.
I continue on.
The dart is in me.

Where is Lord Jesus
When I am sinning?
Does God really see?
The dart is in me.

I want to fit in
This place before me.
The peace I will find.
The dart is in me.

Events around me
To keep me busy.
It is about me.
The dart is in me.

I do no walking
And talking to God.
My dusty Bible.
The dart is in me.

I want all of life.
Need comfort too.
I feel God is pleased.
The dart is in me.

See all I do God.
I want to tell all.
God does love me so.
The dart is in me.

Note: Satan's fiery darts.

The Lie

A tender lie is still a lie
Even when to lessen the pain.
There is a need to be truthful
I'll be honest in all I do.

I do not want brutal truth too,
Especially when I am down.
There needs to be a better way
Than a lie to get me through.

Love is never really easy,
For I am driven like the sea.
As much as I do want this love,
My lie can cause someone else pain.

Christ does want me to worship Him.
Jesus had never lied to me.
Today there is strife I do see
Due to finding out open lies.

Water never stops moving downward
Just like life shall never slow down.
Simple lies do flow on downward
Just to make life complicated.

Many dreams I do possess
Are to make myself to look good.
This can be a wish or a lie.
My Jesus, Your Word is the Truth.

I want to be a follower
Of my Savior Lord Jesus.
Lies cannot be a part of me
To be a true follower, God.

Why did I lie to lessen pain?
I think it would make them happy.
Less heartless by using white lies.
God, I got to stop my lying.

The Thoughts of Life

Jesus went to the mountain
To be alone with Father.
Jesus needed space from crowds;
He needed to talk to Father.

God, let us worship You now.
Let us get alone to pray.
Jesus our example too,
Comes by this simple lesson.

This lesson of not to stop
Talking to our Abba Father.
We share with our God our own love.
And we show Him by our action.

Redeemer Jesus come now.
Satisfied to sin no more.
Looking up the Words of Life
Holy Bible together.

Welcome people in the church
Tell them what Jesus has done.
People are now perishing
Without knowing Jesus saves.

What do Christians mean by saved?
You got to know you are lost.
Heading toward fiery hell.
Not knowing God's holiness.

Do find the time to seek light?
There is love shown in the cross.
There is a time to repent.
There is a Risen Jesus.

Jesus is alive always
No tomb could hold Him in.
A broken seal, He got out.
Changing the history now.

People are blind to the truth.
They do not see Jesus Love.
He died for the likes of us.
Can you comprehend this too?

It's Jesus who is truly God.
He had claimed He is "I AM."
The truth that Moses had then.
The God of the Patriarchs.

It's Jesus who is sinless.
Holy and Pure is Jesus.
Not one example is seen
He ever committed a sin.

It's Jesus who cleanses us.
This is His Blood He had used.
Sin cannot be forgiven
If Jesus's blood is not there.

God made a way to be free.
It can start in you today.
Do take off baggage of guilt,
And give your life to Jesus.

Dying is going to come
As the years continuing.
Yesterday seems so close now
As memories do come to pass.

God, He is still with me.
I had times where I felt tried,
Purified and Holiness.
Time had me a grown-up Christian.

When I become Glorified
After my last breath taken,
Heaven will last forever
Worshipping our dear Father.

These Wars

Onward through hard times
Wars do continue
It's all about sin.
Earth is in trouble.

Why cry out to God?
God's Holy Bible
Says wars shall go on,
Yet Christians do pray.

It's Satan's war too.
Remind us God from
Getting used to them.
Just too many wars.

There are stronger arms
From years gone on too.
Technology has
Created weapons.

Do superpowers
Stop and think about
What they created
Needlessly today.

Kill ratio is high.
Atomic bombs are
Designed to kill all.
Who is safe today?

Where is God in this?
This Holy Bible
Tell us the end-times.
It will get worse too.

What do Christians think?
We know where we will
Be when this happens.
Raptured with Jesus.

This True God

Holy Father
Open my heart,
For God is Good
To come to me.

Jesus the Son
Open my heart.
Father's plan is
Our only Way.

Holy Spirit
Open my heart.
My body is
God's temple.

He is One God
Do remember
This from now on,
The Trinity.

Life is about
Understanding
Myself today
In Christ Jesus.

Above all else,
Place Jesus first
Place in your life
Your neighbor next.

Loving Jesus
Without stopping.
Falling away
Will lead to hell.

In my own life,
Jesus brings peace.
Anyone else
There is conflict.

Savior Jesus,
You are my Lord.
Through Your grace
You save my life.

I do have faith,
Wonderful God.
My life is so
Joyfully filled.

There is a heaven
Jesus prepares
For me to go
And be with Him.

We know Jesus
Went to the Cross.
This fact can change
A lost sinner.

My Comforter,
Holy Spirit.
I stay on the
Holy Bible.

It is the Blood
Of Jesus Christ
Washing away
All my own sins

Touched by Jesus

The Lord's touch is very good;
He is showing us so much.
Jesus wants relationships
From all He's done in our lives.

Worship, loving each today;
We want to be touched by God.
Praise the wonderful Jesus
Every saved and lost soul.

Loving our Jesus with hope
The cross is a touch away.
Resurrection forever
Showing God's Son lives onward

Singing with a touch from God,
Continuing to be joyful.
Jesus opening our hearts
By praising and worshipping.

Touching by healing us so
Jesus who does miracles.
He shows where to find scripture.
This is the Holy Bible.

Discipleship with others
To touch us to show Jesus.
God's moving in our own lives
God's will for us to go out.

Holding on to Lord Jesus
Who is just a touch away.
He does not withhold seeing
Us at the open doorway.

Asking God to touch the sick
Jesus does heal them who come
Physically and mentally.
Spiritual healing does come.

Two Kingdoms

I do place Jesus
Above the world
The world system
Is run by Satan.

Freedom, not bondage,
Comes from my Jesus
The bondage, Satan,
Comes to unsaved lives.

Christians are Jesus's
Children forever
The lost are Satan's
Domain forever.

Christians are now saved
And are heaven bound
Unbelievers are lost
Souls going to hell.

He does love, Jesus,
Comes by Grace and Blood?
He does hate, Satan,
Comes with lies and strife

Jesus is the Way
To reach the Father
Satan is the way
The lost shall follow.

The Holy Spirit,
Jesus gives Christians
Many lost demons,
Satan gives to lost.

Master Jesus has
Resurrected life
Loser Satan has
His fallen angels.

Use Me

God's Grace is upon me.
I'm happy Jesus Christ.
I know how lost I was.
Redeemed by Jesus's love.

God's time is my time too.
Holy Bible does speak
About staying true, God.
You know I want You more.

I will write truthfully
About what You do mean
To me as my Savior.
Show me where I am wrong.

Why does God keep me here?
I sometimes wonder, God.
If I am to be here,
Help me to show You, God.

This short period of life
Is to let people know
There is a God who cares.
He'll never leave us alone.

There's times I disobeyed.
Your presence faded then.
Forgive me God my sins,
And use me Lord today.

Take what little I have.
Let me now to go out.
Physically, I can't.
Use my poetry now.

Holy Spirit is right.
He guides me to Jesus.
God does not stop moving
Even when I pass away.

Want To

Want to sing a song
To Jesus my Lord
Every chance
I get to love Him.

Want to praise each day
For another time
Of spending my time
With Jesus Christ.

Want to thank my God
For all He has done
In my life I live
Given to my Savior.

Want to pray to God
Each day of the week
By finding a place
Of quietness with Him.

Want to give to God
Myself to obey
The words of Bible
Teaching of Jesus.

Want to listen to
The one whom does speak
To my heart each day
Teaching me to hear.

Want to hold on to
Jesus whom changed me
From being a sinner
To be redeemed.

Want to be in faith
In my Lord Jesus
Who is the Author
And the Finisher.

Want to lift my arms
Upward to Jesus
For He is worthy
Of adoration

Want to obey God
With a yes to Him
In doing His Will
In my daily life.

Want to walk with God
Studying His Word
Continuing onwards
To reach Jesus's goals.

Want to seek for lost
Souls who need Jesus
And to be saved
Turning away sin

Want to be present
When the time will come
When I make a choice
To not run away

Want to confess to
My Lord and my God
Jesus about sin
That comes from me.

Want to teach others
Discipleship with
Holy God today
By using Bible.

Want to live for God
Using all of my
Own gifts and all of
My own talents too.

What Further Reason?

What further reason
If I live a life
Filled with good deeds?
My actions feel right.

I help people out
When they need a hand.
It is better to have
Two to solve problem.

I feel happy to
Cheer people on.
It is moments like
This that life goes on.

Do smile to people
Put love in their heart.
Moments of bringing
Laughter in their lives.

Welcome to my house
To be company.
Eat a good meal on
Me while we do talk.

Look for the goodness
In people's hard lives.
Encourage together
To be nice today.

Time do get shorter
As days go on by.
Death may come to friends
Whom I shall miss too.

What about Jesus?
I heard he is God.
An important man
Who did charity.

What's Up

I ask forgiveness if I offend;
Sorry if my thoughts were wrong.
I am human who does not know all.
A sinner redeemed by Holy God.

I'm what God has given me nowadays
A desire to know Jesus better.
Approved by God with my loving Him,
And I'll be more like Jesus Christ.

I'm not interested in being great
Making a name for myself, people.
My actions and my desires are His
From my heart that says, "I'm loving God."

God had delivered me from sinning
When I look upon Jesus my Lord.
Actions continued after I'm saved.
My examples are to read the Word.

I claim the promises of Jesus
He will help me to be a Christian.
I will mind Him and be a person
Whom continues on as God's child.

I believe in Jesus as my Lord.
There are times I need forgiveness.
Do change me Lord to Your likeness.
Hold me, defend me against Satan.

If I do not hold your opinion,
I can still fellowship with you.
Each Christian has the Holy Spirit
To show and to help us understand.

Do explain to me very clearly
What is wrong if I do not see it.
I cannot stop learning more of God
Whom has all the greatest knowledge.

Why Do I Sin On?

I have dreams of God's Way
Do not let my sins stay.
I'll obey my Lord God
With the choices I make.

My defense is Jesus
Blood that he bled for me,
Tokened, cleaned, and freed me.
He gave me His True Peace.

Why grace and not my works?
Grace is faith He gave me.
Works I did on my own
Cannot replace God's grace.

True living came one day
At the altar sins did lay.
My life can become free
From going back to sins.

What is the use I stood
In bondage of my sins.
I know from experience
Sins draws me away, God.

If I fight against sins,
Why do I choose to do?
Let me stop excuses
On my going to sin.

Lord, make me radical
To fight my sins away.
I'll do this, I will fight.
I keep my God in front.

God's will for me, obey
God's will from the Bible.
Sorry God if I'm weak
Strengthen me I do pray.

With Jesus

Love Jesus whom you're with;
Take time to worship Him.
Spend your time when you can
Talking to Holy God.

Adore Jesus today
He will fill your own needs.
God is worthy of all
Praise and all prayers.

Study God's Holy Word
To be approved by Him.
Correctly find the correct way
To scriptures in Bible.

Jesus does never fail
He is God with no sin.
It is now to stop the
Sin in our daily lives.

Jesus, our example
To follow in our lives.
A Christian is to be
Christlike in what we do.

When life gets very tough,
We keep Jesus closer.
He'll strengthen the people
In coping with living.

When things go very wrong,
Hold on to Jesus the
Anchor in our storms.
Run to God in this day.

Strife does not come from God;
We get our lives off God.
Help us, God, to live in
Peace with fellow Christians.

Wrong Life to Right Life

Too much noise in my life!
It is like I do have
To find more to be me,
Especially, wrong life?

Too busy to find time!
It is like I do have
To seek more action too,
Especially, wrong life?

Too crazy as I try!
It is like I do have
To be faster than all,
Especially, wrong life?

Too lost cause in my life!
It is like I do have
To know I am far gone,
Especially, wrong life?

Too young or way too old!
It is like I do have
To let me to move on,
Especially, wrong life?

Too worried to care more!
It is like I do have
To look at wrong ideas,
Especially, wrong life?

Too blue in the bad times!
It is like I do have
To have better times soon,
Especially, wrong life?

Too late to find my way!
It is like I do have
To arrive or lose it,
Especially, wrong life?

Too mad at my own life!
It is like I do have
To find out who I am,
Especially, wrong life?

Too marry or not to!
It is like I do have
To find if I should try,
Especially, wrong life?

Too drunk to really care!
It is like I do have
To stop any more pain,
Especially, wrong life?

Too lost to be myself!
It is like I do have
To find out who I am,
Especially, wrong life?

Too wrong for too long!
It is like I do have
Sin I do see in me,
Especially, wrong life?

Too loved by Jesus Christ!
It is like I do have
Hope to have God's Love,
Especially, right life?

Too moved I am now!
It is like I do have
To turn to my Jesus,
Especially, right life?

Too saved to turn away!
It is like I do have
To never sin again
Especially, right life?

Yourself or Reality

Where is the party at?
Life is given to Satan
On this widen road I follow.
This may bring happiness now?

Imagination is faulty
When I believe God likes sin.
This is I who does want to sin,
For I do for a time like it.

I like and I think my sins
Are pleasing in their own way.
I do receive my pleasures
That I do say I am God's.

Simple man such as I am,
Why give to a God my fun?
There is pain in my life,
Yet alcohol fills my life.

Do not bother this sinner.
I want life to be mine.
I do know life is not right.
I do know what I'm doing.

Nobody likes to be old,
Especially this sinner.
I drink my drinks to Satan
We will have one in hell.

Someday, I will go to God
Before I die, I'll receive.
It's my bet on being safe.
Someday, I'll go to Jesus.

I wish I get more money,
Then happiness will follow.
I do never have enough
I sometimes illegally get.

Pick me up my Lord Jesus
When I do fail so often
Fill me and mold me, Jesus.
Thank you for a sinless life.

I shall live for Lord Jesus,
Even when life seems so hard.
Peace comes in worshipping God
With my faith and my love.

I have true faith in Jesus
By choosing a sinless life.
My witness is in Jesus
By the grace God has given.

If I sin with my own faith,
I will receive my own ways.
God's grace can be taken lightly
By all who keeps on sinning.

Why do the days keep going on
Without delay in my wrongness?
Let me mature in my faith.
Holy Spirit moves my soul.

Life's important, I witness.
It is to be this way now.
Jesus gives me His power
To show others own love.

Holy is my Father God too.
God did send His only Son.
He forever kept me His
By what Jesus did on the cross.

Master God, I will obey,
Teacher, Maker, and Abba
Jesus, my true way to God.
He is first in my own life.

Do I Belong

Farther away from God, I'm so longing
I had searched for something to hold on to.
My own life was without Father God.
I am in this wicked world, I'm sinning.

I had looked for love. What is life about?
In bondage, I'm uncontrolled. I need something.
Christians say there is a God who does care.
In my struggles, just who is this Jesus?

I heard there's a Holy Spirit also.
The Holy Bible has so many wars.
What does this have to do in my sorrows?
Wish to God, He would show Himself to me.

I want to know what Jesus can do now.
I know so little about whom to trust.
This trinity is hard to understand.
I want to know more who He truly is.

"One God!" He said His Creation is Good.
The public school says there's no place for God
Myself, I heard this separation from God.
Evolution, animals above me?

Without God, human life means little too.
I am part of a new generation.
Abortion causes me to be worthless,
Yet I know suicide isn't Jesus's answer.

God and Satan, they have their followers.
Christians, we see in Jesus's death our sins
Upon the wooden Cross at Calvary.
Jesus's resurrection; Satan's own lost

Jesus, Your Father's Love had come to me.
I surrendered to Jesus this moment.
A sanctified life, I do grow onward.
Happiness, I do belong to Jesus.

God Exists

God, I'm forgiven of wickedness
I gave my heart to Jesus Christ.
Before knowing about Jesus,
My ego was not good in life.

God became my deliverer
I'm forever free in Jesus
With the removal of bondage.
Holy God, I've stopped sinning.

Jesus, I am not searching now
You are the only one I want.
Other gods I wondered after.
They can never take Jesus place.

Being me did not satisfy
Every person shall not be
Continuing onward to Heaven.
Especially myself too.

Drifting onward makes life harder
Bible Christians have Jesus Christ.
These ideas that gods shall exist
Cannot replace my emptiness.

My soul has onward existence
Time cannot be reversed by me.
This causes Holy God judgments.
Why did I reject Lord Jesus?

It's written, God's Holy Bible;
Do not leave me Jesus, alone?
Thank you, Father God, for Jesus.
This life I cling to Him closely.

Jesus, living or dead, I'm Yours.
I want a relationship with You.
I exist to love Holy God.
My God is truly forever.

Last Time

Last time to receive Jesus.
Do go to Him as I tell,
For to be saved is right now
Another time may be gone.

Today never be the same.
Christians shared the gospel then.
I said, "I will decide soon
At another date in time."

Life may go on for some time.
I say I have time to choose.
Your death shattered away
By dying without Jesus.

New life is just beginning;
Hell is truly real today.
The demons of hell shall bring
Torment, anguish forever.

Nobody to give you hope,
For Jesus was shun that day.
Your choice came without Jesus.
You are still in your own sins.

I am thinking, I do have some
Family members sinning,
And chooses "no" to Jesus.
I have to show Holy God.

In many ways, easy to
Show to strangers than loved ones.
Strangers and family needs
Jesus while I do witness.

Death and hell together will
Be put in the Lake of Fire.
There shall be no escaping
This fate if died without God.

My Thoughts

Give up old life for new life in God
Are Christians who are New Creations.
A wannabe clowning around is
Not real in being very Holy.

If you do dance like nobody else,
This may be a sign you can't dance.
Just like acting very good like Christians.
This may be a sign you're lost without God.

Do not give up on serving Jesus,
Unlike a person wanting himself.
A true servant of God stands out.
They never did want the lights on them.

God reached you one day long ago.
This made you never want the old man.
Satan's reaches out to ungodly
Where you never wanted Jesus Christ.

Christians, they really like their jobs too?
Those who do the will of Jesus.
Lost ones, many really hate their jobs
Them whom does the will of the devil.

Do you know Christians who has Truth
Within this world they do live in?
Have you ever seen the lost people die
Without Lord Jesus who have ruined lives?

Who says that the Christians have no fun?
Probable drug dealers without hope.
They believe in partying at times,
Especially after they get their fix.

Brothers and sisters loved Lord Jesus,
In Christ, the promised one came to us.
Satan's dominions aren't lovely
As the saying goes, "they accept all."

And Now Sin

And now I dance. Sin!
I am not kidding.
Suggestive movements.
They're rock and rolling.

And now I drink. Sin!
Hard liquor and beer.
Stupidity now.
Much debauchery.

And now I smoke. Sin!
A lit cigarette,
Or illegal joint.
So much foolishness.

And now I peek. Sin!
Use my own body.
Pornography now.
I have to have sex.

And now I rape. Sin!
Pornography now.
Body is exposed.
Disrespect yourself.

And now I cuss. Sin!
A true foul mouther.
Want to be big too.
What you got to prove?

And now I fight. Sin!
Domestic violence.
Uncontrolled anger.
Locked up in a jail.

And now I die. Hell!
Unless forgiven
By Lord Jesus Christ,
This is a true place.

How Do the Lost Surrender?

How do the lost surrender?
Our acts do defy Jesus.
The world has its enticements.
In time, there is no caution.

How do the lost surrender?
Many do continue life
With Satan's own deception.
There is only one True God.

How do the lost surrender?
As ups and downs continue,
It can harden our memories
Of a wicked lonely life.

How do the lost surrender?
Time is sometimes merciless.
Death is in society.
No answers on our aging.

How do the lost surrender?
With open invitation,
Christians are witnessing on
To the lost masses, Jesus.

How do the lost surrender?
Holy Spirit does show us
The Father's Crucified Son.
Let the love continue on.

How do the lost surrender?
Our works will not save ourselves.
Jesus had shed His own blood
Jesus's grace can be our grace.

How do the lost surrender?
It is between God and you.
Decisions to follow God
Comes by our own surrender.

A Pretender in Church

People looking to do good,
Yet Sunday they do try to
Make it to their church.
Respectable thing to do.

They do things for Jesus
Yet when they think about it,
They'll once in a while begin
To open a Holy Bible.

They call Jesus their Lord,
Yet they please themselves.
Church activities are a
Fun church they search for.

The church people are nice,
Yet they need to get modern.
We'll be sure to inform them
Of better ways to improve all.

They do listen to the preacher,
Yet we want to get home
For Sunday's sport announcers.
Got to find out my team's strengths.

They want a clock on church wall,
This way they will remind the
Pastor how long he preached.
A routine we must have now.

Fashionable to be late to church,
Yet they are first to get out too.
They have no hunger in them
For a time to be with Jesus.

God is knocking on hearts' door,
Yet they are proud in their lives.
They know not what Church
Is all about Holy God today.

A Simple Man

In Proverbs, a simple man
Is a man enticed by a
Sexual relationship.
Do not fall for her advances.

He's easily drawn into
A woman's body of lust.
He does not see the whole deal.
Will you go to hell someday?

This does not please Holy God.
The man is far away where
He willingly went unto Her.
She'll drew him away from God.

This is Satan's ideal too.
Mankind does say the man had
Got lucky being with her.
Are you willing to be dumb?

This very day many problems
Can arise by diseases.
Even some may fall ill too.
World say, use a condom.

There was a time I was drawn
Into a woman's open
Arms enticing me in this act.
A few drinks, and it happened.

This did not satisfy me.
I felt like Satan was glad.
My relationship with God
Stopped over a loose woman.

Do not laugh at my own poem
Taken from God's Holy Word.
God really means what He says.
Do willingly stop sinning.

Active God

Talk to the Lord
Every day.
Tell about Love
Of the Lord's way.

Walk with Jesus
Along the path.
Know Jesus Christ
Personally.

We want Jesus
To show us now.
I believe Him
From the Bible.

Make up your mind
On loving God.
Lead me today
To serve Jesus.

Obedience
Is better Lord
When we do pray
For Your own Way.

Keep me to see
The needs of all,
Especially
Other Christians.

I don't forget
The wooden Cross.
You had told us
To remember.

Do not let me
Disobey God.
Our Jesus blood
Washed us clean.

Ask to be whole
In Jesus the
Messiah of
The true Bible.

Follow Jesus's
Own example.
This is to be
Christlike today.

Listen to God's
Very own Son.
Father sent Him.
Will we hear God.

Give to God your
Attention
When the teacher
Expounds the Word.

We praise Father,
Jesus the Son, and
Holy Spirit,
For He is Good.

Thank you, my Lord
Jesus for each
And every
Blessing You give.

All You Need Is Jesus

Anybody can come
All you need is Jesus.
He says, "I am the Door."
Will all come in to God?

He wants our hearts today
All you need is Jesus.
He says, "Faith is unseen,"
And grace makes us welcomed.

What is people's concern?
All you need is Jesus.
He says, "Now is the time,"
Do not delay today.

Decisions to be free
All you need is Jesus.
He says, "Come to me"
Take your first step now.

Our sins are rebellion
All you need is Jesus.
He says, "This is the day"
When we change our own lives.

Our times get so busy
All you need is Jesus.
He says, "I am the Way"
God will give you His time.

Our ways are so wicked
All you need is Jesus.
He says, "I am the vine"
He will bring you this peace.

People are dying now
All you need is Jesus.
He says, "Carry your Cross"
We must do God's Will.

Appearances

I will be happy.
See how good I am.
Today, I will do
What I feel is right.

Love is my motto.
Where can I find it?
People see my deeds
And think it is good.

I am an owner
Of a business.
Compliments I want.
I need my respect.

I'm glad to see a
Smile on their face,
Especially from
The opposite sex.

Church is where I need
To show people me.
Just how well life is.
Good for my ego.

Sunday morning, I
Put on my best clothes.
They see how well I
Am doing today.

Found a minister
Who makes me feel good
About myself too.
Power is my goal.

Buddy, you are wrong.
Christian relationship
With Lord Jesus Christ
Is what you do need.

Bless Me

Bless me, God, so I can do more for others
With all that you give me to give with love.
In Your Holy and Precious name, Jesus,
Give me a right heart and a right attitude.

Sometimes I do wonder if I should ask Jesus
To bless my prayers, worship, and time.
I do not believe in the world's health and
Wealth message some pastors endorse.

God is a giver to them whom loves Him.
One song says, "You cannot outgive God."
I do believe this is a true and right idea.
This song is the central truth of Christianity.

God owns it all, my life, my hopes, and my love.
I am made in His own image, thank you, Jesus.
I am made to give everything to my Lord.
I have a relationship I'm still growing into.

I want Jesus more each passing day and night.
Why does God allow Satan run this world?
Jesus pulled me out of my own wickedness
Lifestyle in this world full of Satan's corruption.

He made me a Christian that chooses to not sin.
My choice is to obey God with everything.
Jesus gave me so much that I say "God blessed me."
I will never be the same before I came to Christ.

I'm blessed to seek God's will for my own life.
Thank you, Father, for sending Your Son for me.
Holy Spirit keeps me center on living Holy.
I want to be a Christian others see a difference.

The reason I am a Christian is Jesus Christ from
God's Holy and Blessed written Word in Bible.
I place my life in Jesus's hands forever and ever.
I surrender my life to be living for Jesus's Love.

Candle under a Bottle

Candle under a bottle
Will go out when it's lit
Just like our path light out
As Christians going out.

Then Satan will have his
Field day of joy today
He stirs up mischief in
Our lives we live right now.

This is due to taking
It easy as possible
Without any conflict.
No conflict, no troubles.

No troubles, all quiet.
Are we now in the war
Against Satan and God?
Do let your light shine on.

If your light has gone out,
Christians cannot fight on.
What Jesus says is life.
Our lives are God given.

Do keep God first in life.
We are to stay on path.
If we get off the path,
Come back to Jesus Christ.

On which road will you take?
Either we live for God,
Or you live for Satan.
These two are the results.

God helps to open eyes.
Do light up the candle
And not put the light out.
Then may we go witness.

Christian Music

Play the Christian music
That uplifts my own soul.
Jesus, You are my own
Inspiration today.

Special singers do have
Voices that make me see
More of heaven will be
Like when I do get there.

Piano and organ
Music starts me to be
Ready for the rest of
The service I am in.

Instruments bring out
More of God's blessing to
My soul and my heart,
Especially in church.

Talents do come out in
The service I am in.
Church is to continue
To reach out to the lost.

Music to me is God's
Special Christian talents
Moved by Holy Spirit.
They sing unto the Lord.

The words in the singing
Bring out the messages
Of the Gospel also.
Thank you, my Holy God.

The invitation to lost
Brings out moving words
That tell the people come.
Praise Jesus my soul.

Closer to God

I ran fast, I was young.
I was so very lost.

I had searched, is God real?
I had thought for so long.

Jesus Christ, my Savior
I am New Creation.

A slower walk, middle age.
My time to get knowledge.

Not to swift, older age.
I feel closer to God.

Worship God, pray each day.
My love to Jesus Christ.

Follower, True Christian.
I'm in the Book of Life.

My God's good my faith strong.
I will be glorified.

Heaven bound, entrance.
I'll meet Jesus my Lord.

Enter in, grace and blood.
My own faith in Jesus.

Crises

Where is the church people?
In our nation's crisis
God knows all about us.
Jesus is stability.

Lost people need Jesus.
The lost and the saved need
Spiritual guidance.
Only Jesus can guide.

Jesus is the true way.
The everlasting peace
Comes when you're delivered.
The world causes problems.

Jesus hung at Calvary.
He obeyed the Father.
Jesus took all sins then.
Give your life to Jesus.

Sins are depravity.
No request, commandment
Surrender to Jesus
And ask for forgiveness.

You will never find peace
If you do not go to
The One whom gives us peace.
The is our Lord Jesus.

Transgression in Crises
Caused many problems too.
People turn to God then.
After crises, they forget.

No matter what this life
Does brings upon Christians,
We know Jesus is the
Answer to the crises.

Cruel

The lost people, move
Without salvation
In this cruel world
Satan is ruling.

God does move, run
From sinning onward.
Cruel death Jesus had
On Calvary Cross.

True Christians, we are
Believers in God
In this cruel time
Surrounding the lost.

Unbelievers, God
Shall be a judge.
Hell is a cruel place
Where the lost shall go.

Please, pastors, teach us
To go and to reach.
It is cruel to not
Warn people today.

Congregations, why
Sit in the same seat?
Unaware how cruel
People perishing.

Father God, we pray
To be used by You
No cruel actions now,
But Love of Jesus.

Jesus Christ, Christians
Know you are our peace,
We were once cruel,
Yet now we are Yours.

Don't Know

On this side, you see.
On that side, I hide.
When I try to be,
God knows me too well.

What am I to do?
One will think of this.
One will think of that.
I do not know God.

One is satisfied.
One is not happy.
I'm caught in the middle.
God, I seek Your help.

One day I explain.
One day I'm silent.
Where do I stand now?
God, You understand.

God, like the weather,
It does change often.
I leave it with You.
I just do not know.

Thank God for Bible.
It says what God says.
It's in our language.
There I do now know.

Early Life

God, all my childhood
I knew You were Holy.
Kids club was very good.
I knew God was special.

Life was not kind to me.
Only myself I knew
Not what life was about.
Lifestyle of many lies.

Where was I headed to?
Unpleasing was normal.
Many days I knew I
Needed more than myself.

I tried to find a mate.
I changed them my own way.
This is truly my hell
I knew in my own mind.

Who shall follow me on?
Babies, they were born now.
It brings to me meaning.
Life after death moves on.

How can I stop aging?
Death shall someday come.
I do not want to die.
Will life stop forever?

My childhood memory
Of Jesus's love for me.
Was this life all for me?
I burnt many bridges.

Jesus of childhood.
A memory I had.
A life that was easy.
Can He be my God now?

False Evolution

Eternity started further
Than any time we can think of
The Trinity God was present
Always in time that never ends.

God had made Adam and Eve
In the image we are today.
Evolution is a lie from
Satan, the fallen angel.

Evolution is people's way
To replace our God's Creation.
Evolution wants mankind
To be the way people should think.

False says the Christians today.
With this idea we came from
Being nothing into something,
In which, defies scientific laws.

All Evolution theory is
An idea mankind has to
Replace Holy and True Jesus.
Evolutionists are atheist.

Why does Evolution stay in
The public school system?
They want to get rid of God today.
This is the atheist belief.

Creation is an easier
Belief than Evolution too.
Evolution does not make sense
They have no evidence that stands.

We start in the Holy Bible
To see Scripture is the Truth.
Our Christian faith is not blind
Faith like Evolution stands on.

God's Way

He made me whole to be used
Because Jesus is my God.
His will is what I do want
Personal relationship.

I do believe that Jesus
The Messiah of the Bible
The prophets had spoken of
He is the Fulfillment One.

Nobody but Lord Jesus
Will judge the wicked people.
He will welcome the righteous
Ones given their hearts to God.

Christians know the Bible
That shows us what Jesus want.
This is a clear message too.
Our God's grace does save people.

Why don't unsaved people stop
Wanting more of something?
This is a miserable life
Some commit suicide too.

Go out Christian today
To tell them God's message
Of hope for their lost lives.
Thank God many are going.

Who but God gets happy
When a soul comes to Him.
Praise the Lord all people,
And thank you Holy Spirit.

Holy Spirit works on the
Unsaved lives by using us.
Christians do come in their lives
To help them see the Way.

God Does Know

Easy or hard questions,
Jesus will answer them.
In time, I will see it
Was handled by Jesus.

Time in my opinion
With God's Holy Bible,
There will come Jesus's peace
Upon my life of changes.

I just wish for Jesus
To continue teaching
Me ways to cope within
Circumstances I'm in.

Misunderstandings are
Hard to see true peace
Because people are not
Keeping in mind Your Ways.

I am not the perfect one.
Jesus truly is God
Who is always perfect
In all His own actions.

I do trust in Jesus
Working to smooth edges
Within my ways sometimes
I handle situations.

God does understand me
More than what I do see.
Submission to Jesus
Is at the core today.

I forgive and forget.
I do not want to be
Far away from Jesus.
I let God handle it.

God's Wisdom

Godly truth in God
Is all that's needed.
Why do we believe
Not a Holy God?

The world does not see
How God moves within
All of life's questions,
God already knows.

Jesus is speaking
It's the Word of God.
He's God incarnate.
The Word is written.

The unbelievers
Always lack wisdom.
The believers are
Growing and learning.

Our Christian wisdom
Starts when we are saved.
Bible, it's the way
Holy Spirit moves.

Non-Christians are to
Leave Jesus outside.
Many times they do
Laugh at Jesus Christ.

Mankind mocks the Word
That God is so good.
Words flow blasphemes
Cursing at Jesus.

Pray for true wisdom
As God does show us.
He is generous
With the Word of God.

False wisdom teaches
More about yourself.
The Humanists says
Mankind is wisdom.

Mankind created
More hatred within
Core of their being,
A godless world.

Man's wisdom leads to
Satan's own forces.
Man can be a god
Man will solve problems.

God is so alive
We will worship Him.
Wisdom is alive
God gives it freely.

Wisdom from Bible
Is the way to go.
Deal kindly to them
Who does seek it so.

Value True God now.
Study to be right
In your own thinking
How everything works.

Thank you, my Jesus.
Wisdom is so free.
It cost only time
Spent in the Bible.

Disagree with this
Poem that goes to God.
Wisdom begins here.
Mankind is fallen.

Godly Christian Beliefs

We need, yet many don't have.
Second Blessing, we need it.
"There's no hurry," Satan says.
Why do you need His advice?

We sin no more willfully,
For we must all die to self.
We're running a race today,
Keep our eyes on finishing.

Our God will not be so hard
Never will He send us out,
Except love, without a hell.
Christians know this is not truth.

There needs to be a New Birth,
Wholly Sanctified,
And continued maturing.
Christians need to strive for this.

Means that you must sin no more
For sin does depress us so.
If we sin, ask forgiveness.
Father sent a living Son.

Some Christians think we must sin.
This is also very false.
You choose to, or you choose not.
At New Birth you stop sinning.

We believe His Grace, His Blood,
And His Faith leads onward.
We teach others salvation
Comes to us by Jesus Christ.

We start out as new babies
Where the Bible is so taught.
As the time pass us on by,
We should mature gracefully.

God's Holiness

Holiness comes from God.
An important reason
To ask Jesus for it
For Jesus is Holy.

We get Holy when we
Surrender our old ways
Of our carnal nature.
We must die to our sins.

It is not good feelings
Of our inner nature
Making us holier.
Jesus is our example.

Many holy people
Do go God's Narrow Way.
We grow and we mature
With Jesus in our lives.

People moves towards self.
It is not enough now
To do it without God.
Jesus's Holiness lives.

Time is not on your side,
For life is like the mist
That the Sun shines on.
Go to Holy God now.

Sin had come from Adam
Sin is removed by God.
This is when we give our
Lives totally to God.

I cannot stress this more.
Holiness is the way.
How do we get holy?
Jesus is our example.

God's Way

When saved, Holy Spirit came
To me while I was at the altar
I did not have to go out
And seek to find Holy God.

As for Second Work of Grace,
I was made Sanctified Wholly.
I am maturing in God
Every day of my life.

I waited for Holy God
In my prayers each day.
Speak to me, God, as I do
Give my love to Jesus Christ.

Thank you for talking to me,
Reading the Holy Bible.
I do wish to know Jesus
More as example in my life.

I praise Jesus's Holy name
Because He is the True Way
To live my life all for God.
I have no new way to go.

My only way is by Grace
I had never worked for this.
My Father sent Jesus.
He took upon Himself sin.

There are valleys and mountains
While living my own life.
These were times I did need God
For both times God was present.

Jesus puts Love into me
The Love only God can give.
Now I do love my Jesus,
Others, and lastly myself.

Happiness

God is my happiness
He who moves my own soul.
I have Jesus to thank
To bring hope within me.

Even in the bad days
When I am not myself,
He brings to me His joy.
Happiness does come back.

I do see God's loving
Workings upon me too.
Times with my Savior
Brings back memories.

Holy Spirit moves too.
Jesus, I am moody.
Father, I do thank you
For I know You are good.

I enjoy spending time
With just my God and I.
Loneliness is when I
Do not allow God in.

As I am in God's Will,
My faith in God does grow.
Holiness unto God,
I know this happiness.

To spend time in Bible,
I feel closer to God.
He makes me so happy.
This helps with sinless life.

My future in heaven
When I run the true race
Is to believe in God.
His place makes me want it.

He Is Jesus

It sometimes escapes
When life seems so fast.
Peaceful is Jesus
He gives to us peace.

Finding time to be
With Jesus my Lord.
Prayerful is Jesus
He has us to pray.

Times are so very
Worried and hurried.
Faithful is Jesus
He gives us our faith.

Take God anytime
At His Holy Word.
Thankful is Jesus
We will always thank.

Sorry are the times
With so much to lose.
Hopeful is Jesus
He gives to us hope.

Lord does work when
We do need His will.
Helpful is Jesus,
He wants us to help.

Do not be fearful
For Jesus was not.
Careful is Jesus
We really do care.

Jesus in my mind
Is someday coming.
Handful is Jesus
We are in His hand.

The times are so good
When I follow God.
Praiseful is Jesus;
We will always praise.

We have family
Who were never saved.
Powerful is Jesus
Give us your power.

Not knowing God's plan
Where He does see all.
Graceful is Jesus
He will give us grace.

God is truly here
So freely loving.
Tearful is Jesus
When we are in tears.

Mighty, Just, and Love
All the time He is.
Mindful is Jesus
He has us in mind.

Take a stand we say
To those who do faint.
Truthful is Jesus.
Jesus knows the truth.

People are looking
Without knowing God.
Merciful is Jesus
We need His mercy.

God's ways are Here
For we are in awe.
Wonderful is Jesus
You're full of wonder.

Grab on to Jesus Christ

God's Yoke is there for us
When our burdens are hard.
Grab on to Jesus Christ
When we do need His help.

God's Son is there for us
When we just want someone.
Grab on to Jesus Christ
When we do pray to God.

God's Grace is there for us
When we want salvation.
Grab on to Jesus Christ
When we do want God' plan.

God's Blood is there for us
When we want to be washed.
Grab on to Jesus Christ
When we have sins removed.

God's Word is there for us
When we know Father's Love.
Grab on to Jesus Christ
When we do grasp this truth.

God's Voice is there for us
When we read Word of God.
Grab on to Jesus Christ
When we believe in God.

God's Strength is there for us
When we do need a hand.
Grab on to Jesus Christ
When we see God's power.

God's Love is there for us
When we do need Father.
Grab on to Jesus Christ
When we do want loving.

Holy Bible Is the Test

Pure Faith is commanded
From our God whom requires
Everyone to have.
Holy Bible is the test.

What exactly is pure?
It is to live without sin.
Holy Spirit is in us.
Holy Bible is the test.

A clear mind pleasing to God.
Not to be proud in your soul,
Or judgmental in actions.
Holy Bible is the test.

A true heart for Jesus.
Love of your own neighbors.
And yourself last of all.
Holy Bible is the test,

A trust in Holy Father.
He has might and power.
Reach out to Him in Love.
Holy Bible is the test.

Who will go on sinning?
Them who do commit these acts.
Actions based on rebellion.
Holy Bible is the test.

What are Christians to do now?
Show whom is not so holy.
Changes do come from Jesus.
Holy Bible is the test.

God can change a person's life.
He is our own Creator,
Yet He did give free choice.
Holy Bible is the test.

I Bring to God

I do bring to God my worship
My desire to love Him so.
There is peace under my roof.
This Holy God whom does see me.

I do bring to God my prayers
For I continue to believe
On Jesus who does listen
And answer my many questions.

I do bring to Jesus my love
Because I know whom I believe.
He heard me when I needed Him.
How wonderful Jesus does move.

I do bring to Jesus my hope,
For the people all around me,
Especially my family.
Salvation is through Jesus Christ.

I do bring to Jesus my all.
Take my transgressions as I seek
Salvation, I do want you today.
Surrender, God is forever.

I do bring to God my thoughts.
Give to me a right attitude
In plans You have me to do.
Open up to me this true path.

I do bring to God my thanks
With happiness in telling all
How good the ways of knowing God
May my own actions please, Jesus.

I do bring to God my sins,
Yet I am saved, not sanctified.
Sins get me to go against God
I know God wants me not to sin.

I do bring to God my hands
And feet to go out to the souls
The words of a living Savior.
Daily the Holy Spirit moves me.

I do bring to God my life
To be a true Christian who shows
The Living Holy Bible says,
Priesthood of believers today.

I do bring to God my heart
A relationship with Holy God,
Father, Son, and Holy Spirit.
This God wants my obedience.

I do bring to God my songs
Within my being towards God.
My faith expressed in Jesus.
Holy Spirit moves me onward.

I do bring to God my ways.
Nothing holding back from Jesus,
Time, money prayers, and loving.
God does love all due to the cross.

I do bring to God my no "I."
There are some things I do have pride,
Yet I do try not to be proud
In my own sight. God is my all.

I do bring to God my own hurts.
There are times I feel unwanted,
Yet God never does throw me out
I do give to Him my own hurts.

I Love Jesus

I am able Jesus
To stand firmly with You.
It's the way I shall go
Jesus knows my own heart.

People, I am happy
All that God's given me.
It's the way I shall go
Holding on to Jesus.

Every day I pray
The Father through the Son.
I kneel, and I talk to God
That is the way life goes.

Singing songs about God
I listen to the Word.
Jesus is the topic
With His Glorious Love.

Farther along the path
Aging gracefully on,
I see the Trinity,
And this is truly God.

Nowhere but to Jesus
Shall my devotions go
I bring all to Jesus,
And my own humbleness.

Witnessing to others
Along my own journey
Taking all to Jesus.
I shall witness to all.

Praising along with God
What's really in my heart.
Thanking God for his
Own righteousness today.

In This World

God cares, and I care for a
Relationship with Jesus.
A journey I kept faithful
Until I am in heaven.

I had wished I went sooner
To the Cross of Calvary.
I was destined for this hell
Where I had laugh it away.

Mocking and not knowing God
With His holiness today.
I heard a man named Jesus
And wondered if He was pleased.

I'll stand strong in this world
To be the man I am now.
Just who is this Jesus
This world continues to ask.

Do deliver says the world
Do be the man you are now.
Mighty feats and mighty acts
To please my image also.

Shall people remember me
As an ego-pleasing man.
I did my own desires
For all mankind to see me.

Open the Holy Bible now,
Is Jesus the truthful one?
Life is too short to hold on
Hell is no place to live in.

Bless my Christian unity
By the words Jesus does use.
This is forever, Jesus,
And You live in my own heart.

Is This Your Last Chance

Is this your last chance
To be a Christian?
Let me explain just
How important this is.

You feel emptiness
So often in Life.
You tried many things,
Except Jesus Christ.

Is your attitude
I'll do it my way.
Has this brought you peace
Doing it your way.

You're on top of the
Mountain of success.
There will come a time
Life is meaningless.

Life is very short
As you grow older.
The Bible is right
On life being short.

Lost dreams fade on
Into daily life.
If I lived the dream,
Happiness would come.

Can you surrender
To Jesus Christ?
Peace, Jesus does give.
It's worth living on.

Everything to
Gain in Jesus Christ.
Your sins will lead on
Into emptiness.

It Is Forever

It is forever!
Lord, my Savior.
Freed to stop sinning.
The choice is mine.

World actions
Spiritual death.
Violence erupts.
Why delay Jesus?

Are you a Christian?
Jesus is the Way.
God's Blood and God's Grace
Gets relationships.

It's not your mommy
It's not your goodness.
Salvation shall come
Only by Jesus.

Why are we so weak?
Christianity
Is to be showing
The Lord within you.

One day, I be there
To see Lord Jesus.
I'll go to Heaven
Jesus preparing.

Heaven glorified!
What can I tell you?
This plan God given
This race we do run.

A new believer:
A new creation.
It is forever!
Christianity.

Jesus Is for All People

I, myself, need all of Lord Jesus Christ
By worshipping my God every day.
Please move me in Jesus's Holy Name.
I really do want to touch them for God.

My family needs Lord Jesus in their lives.
They who know Jesus are moved too.
They who do not know Jesus save them.
The complacent put them on fire for Him.

My kinsmen or my kinswomen need Jesus.
Hold them in your heart Lord to show them
You are the Almighty one and the Holy one.
Please save my kin today Lord Jesus.

My neighbor does need Jesus also.
Hold them in Your Hands my Lord.
They are going to a place called hell.
They do need God's Jesus to save them.

My county does need Lord's Love for them.
These are our countryside people today.
Let us pray for their salvation to Jesus.
Tell them the message Jesus does save.

My town does need Lord Jesus's Love.
Do become Christlike in telling them
That God's above everyone that comes
Before Him in a town with neighbors.

My city in this country needs Jesus Christ.
Let us keep eyes open to receive Jesus.
Read the Holy Bible as a nation should do.
Move all the people to keep us Christian.

Finally, the world needs Lord Jesus.
The Great Commission is to go out
Into all lands disciples to Jesus Christ.
Praise God we shall speak boldly too.

Jesus's Loving Ways

Why do people blame Holy God?
They do not see Your Loving Ways.
Jesus will be there in bad times,
And He will be present in good times.

He will never leave you alone
In the times you cannot feel God,
He is present beside your side.
Let Him in to comfort your life.

He loved you, and He died for you
There is a void when you go through
Life not knowing Jesus's True Peace.
Days will be like this when you're down.

He will see you through your troubles
Don't give up hope during hard times.
Place your faith in the Living Lord
Jesus been through this as man/God.

He will give you His peace in life
Receive Him into your own heart.
Tell Jesus what is on your mind.
He's a good listener you know.

Listen to Jesus at the times
Of looking for His talking truth.
It does come from a Heart of God.
He does not reject your own pleas.

Do let His Love flow through yourself.
Take time to remember His Word.
Pick up the Bible written by God.
He will speak to me from the Bible.

Believe in God who changes not.
The Bible shows the True Jesus.
The Son of God Father sent us
Because of the Love for His children.

My Goal

What I want to do is read on?
The Old and New Testament Word.
I'll obediently obey.
God had showed me wisdom and strength.

Old Testament teaches Jesus,
And his coming death on the Cross.
Prophets forever serving God;
Each adding picture of Jesus.

New Testament is about Jesus
With God's own Son speaking to us.
This spotless lamb; God had been slain.
Shedding His own blood on the Cross.

This blood that Jesus Crist had spilt
Was filled in the New Testament.
The story of Jesus never ends.
His resurrection, He does live.

This joy Jesus does give to me,
For Jesus spoke he will come back.
He ascended, He will return
On a White Horse full of Glory.

Gone before the tribulation.
I will be going with Jesus.
Many things in tribulation
Shall cause so many people's death.

The Jews will evangelize too,
One hundred forty-four thousand.
Many be given one more chance
To die for Jesus as martyrs.

I will not hold back my praises
This heaven is my goal in life.
It's my own love for Jesus Christ,
Relationship that never end.

My Lord, Jesus

I enjoy God,
My Lord, Jesus.
He makes me say
I love you God.

I know my God,
My Lord, Jesus.
He showed me love
Towards others.

I talk to God,
My Lord Jesus.
He speaks to me
About His life.

I reach out to God,
My Lord, Jesus.
He meets me now,
And not later.

I pray to God,
My Lord, Jesus.
He always hears
My calls to Him.

I sing to God,
My Lord, Jesus.
I lift up God
With my own voice.

I say to God,
My Lord, Jesus.
I thank you God
For being good.

I go to God,
My Lord, Jesus.
He tells me to
Come before Him.

I know my God,
My Lord, Jesus.
He is the True
Three-in-One God.

I speak to God,
My Lord, Jesus.
He is the Truth,
Not any lies.

I hear my God,
My Lord, Jesus.
He is the God
Of the Bible.

I need my God,
My Lord, Jesus.
My concerns are
Open to Him.

I call my God,
My Lord, Jesus.
You reached me
God with Your Word.

I saw my God,
My Lord, Jesus.
I belong to
His Own Kingdom.

I grasp my God,
My Lord, Jesus.
His every
Word I do read.

I pray my God,
My Lord, Jesus.
Open my heart
To tell You all.

No Fun

The fun had lasted until life set in
Why did I say the cause was sinning?
I had lived with a false life I made
Laughed with what I had brought in time.
I had a life many people would want.
Why did my pleasures ended without fun?

I had worked hard to get my experience
In all that I did and thought about now.
The material goods had brought in much fun.
Then onto another game for my life.
I can tear down, and I can build up too.
Why did my pleasures ended without fun?

Nobody understands what I do want
Especially I in my own search.
I've tried so many times to find reason
Lost in a place I do not find the truth.
Eagerly moving without finding me.
Why did my pleasures ended without fun?

Then one day I went to a Christian Church.
The Word from the Holy Bible was heard
Something opened to me what they read.
That was many years ago I heard God.
The ways of God did bring meaning to me.
I did find pleasure with a lot of Fun.

Now

This is now, and that was then.
A Christian man witnessing.
The old man caught up in sin.
Now I'm a new creation.

Christian now and lost was then.
God came into my own heart.
I could not find my own way.
Now I'm living for Jesus.

Truth is now and false was then.
I'm called to be God's child.
I dreamed of finding myself.
Now I'm truly with Jesus.

Life is now and death was then.
I'll go to a place with God.
Going to hell didn't seem real.
Now I tell people it's God.

Grace is now and damned was then.
Grace is only way to Jesus.
Death leads towards fiery hell.
Now I'm accepting His gift.

Love is now and curse was then.
Jesus fills me with His Love.
Cursed was my sins back then.
Now I'm so happy, Jesus.

Faith is now and coward was then.
I felt I could with Jesus.
My early life was very hard
Now my faith is in Jesus.

Christ is now and Satan was then.
Jesus lover of my soul.
I lived too long for Satan.
Redeemed and saved forever.

Old Age

Fast pace doing nothing;
Where does all the time go?
Old age is our story,
Ailments continually.

Family, grandchildren
Where we do love them so?
They make us feel younger.
Seeing them playing their games.

We may not have the speed
We once took for granted.
Blessed to have our place
With many memories.

Doctors, we have many
Sorting pills for the week.
Our children helping us
To make sure we take pills.

Praise our Lord Jesus Christ.
Our prayers go to him.
We do have much time to
Be doing whatever now.

Old people singing songs,
Especially Christian songs.
Piano in nursing home
Playing with much love too.

We may be encourager,
Welcoming and sharing.
This is our own choosing
To be as close to God.

Elderly closer now
As time passes onward.
Heaven is our own goal,
Saved by Jesus's own grace.

Open God

I do serve an open
God amongst the lost.
He is not hard to
Reach in our own lives.

God does reach out to
All people in world.
Open your heart today
For a waiting God.

Father sent His Son
To bring us to Him.
Come to Lord Jesus.
He is Holy and Just.

There is only one
Father's plan today.
The only way to
Father is by Jesus.

Jesus is Savior,
And He is True God.
Jesus the only
Choice people do have.

Oh! Men and women,
Do not let the world
Get your eyes off God.
He lives, Jesus Christ.

He is satisfying,
And He is fulfilling.
Christians are to be
With Holy Spirit.

Why do many stay blind?
It can only be
Satan had deceived
The hearts of mankind.

Pray and Do

I do listen to Jesus
While I shall pray in my chair.
I am in my quiet place.
I do obey my Jesus.

Today, I do read Bible
Where nobody can deny.
I do have the True Scriptures
Where I do see my Jesus.

I do tell Jesus I do love.
I want to tell God always.
He keeps me with His Own Love.
I do want to follow on.

God is my own advocate
Because Satan wants my life.
Father, I know Jesus has pardoned
I stopped sinning.

I have Jesus's own justice.
Nobody else can give me.
Yes, court cases do go on,
Yet True Peace comes from Jesus.

Election—this is God's way.
He knew me before I lived.
He chose me to be Christian.
My choosing I made myself.

God's directions in this life
Is through the Holy Bible
Prophets and Apostles,
God gave to faithful people.

Do move me Holy Spirit.
I want to stay with Jesus.
I shall go to lost people
Where True Spirit does go out.

Rejected and Tired

Early one morning
Writing poetry,
God, help them today
To find happiness.

Their life they do live
With many around,
They look for something
Worth living for.

Their daily routine
They had set up
Runs throughout the week
Without knowing God.

Somewhere in the dark
Still cleaning to hope
For a better life
They do never reach,

Rejected and tired
Not to understand
No peace in their lives
They continue onward.

The faster the day,
More hurried life is.
In their existence,
It's start to finish.

Can Jesus be real?
Would He see me too?
God does really care
In this world we live.

Jesus will bring peace.
Peace not found in world,
Yet in God's own grace
Is forgiveness of sins,

Right Way or Wrong Way

One day is too much
When sin comes along.
I does not matter
On what sins you do.

Do more to not sin
By allowing God
To cleanse your life.
Go not back to sin.

Sin is like a snake
That has bitten you.
The sin develops
Into your own death.

Total obedience.
This is God's command
This is not a wish,
Read Holy Bible.

Father sent to us
His only one Son.
Jesus did obey,
Calvary story.

There may come a day
When your life changes
Into the person
Who follows Jesus.

Only in Jesus
Is mankind found to
Go to Father God
Up into Heaven.

Father, Son on right
And Holy Spirit
Moving the redeemed,
Trinity is true.

If God is what we
Want to make God be,
Our own ways are wrong.
This is Satan lies.

Worthy is Jesus
Who was slain back then.
Jesus obeyed when
The cost was the Cross.

What's in it for me,
Says the people who
Will bring in the bucks.
Wolves who do get.

Most pastors do live
Within their own means.
They are not so rich,
Yet God does supply.

He supplies our needs
According to the Bible,
Not monetary.
It's being with God.

Let us make a deal,
Says the unsaved one.
God will not bargain
For lost sinners souls.

Do be true to God
Give your heart to God.
Jesus will save you.
From your wicked sins.

How is your service?
How can we obey
All that is in us?
Simple, obey God.

Salvation Now

As I reached to find
The answers today,
My faith required
Me to save my soul.

They told their message
To be saved by grace.
Today they had said,
"Go to Jesus now."

Father allowed this.
Jesus took on sins
Of the whole world
While on the Cross.

They did many things
On Friday the day
He hung on the Cross.
They tortured Jesus.

On the third day, Sunday,
Jesus had risen.
Alive and well too,
Not to die again.

Finally, I asked,
"What else in Bible?"
"It never does end,"
Said the True Christian.

God, forgive my sins.
I shall do right now.
Salvation message
Presented to me.

I do accept God
Lord and Savior.
Jesus you are mine.
I will go forward.

Satan's Idols

People place many things
Before a Holy God.
Beware of little gods
Where they are all around.

What comes between Jesus
Takes our time away, God?
These old desires are
As old as time we know.

World says gods are new,
But they are not so new.
In times past the people
Try to replace our God.

Jesus is our True God.
Atheists see no God.
Agnostics do not know.
The people live for self.

Ourselves is the "I" god.
Where is present Jesus?
They do hate what is good.
Why do they love the bad?

Nobody likes to be
Told what to do, Father.
They laugh at the Christians
Whom believes in Jesus.

Satan wants the people
To worship him only.
He fights against our Lord.
Bitter is the loser.

Disgusted, Satan has
To acknowledge Jesus.
He will be defeated
According to the Word.

What do we do with God?
This choice of idolatry
Moves us away from God.
Our God does never change.

The Bible tells the truth.
Father, Jesus, and the
Holy Spirit tells us
There is only one God.

Why are people dying
With the Holy Bible
On their own night table
By never reading it.

Satan wants, due to hate,
People who are condemned
By a Holy Just God.
This Lake of Fire is true.

Forbidden in Heaven,
Lost people will not be
Comforted by Father.
Lost souls will be in hell.

Their idols above God
Got to be their reward
Because the choice they made
Where Jesus never changed.

Take Satan seriously.
People now want to joke.
This is okay with him.
They belong to Satan.

Satan's Idols never
Got anyone to God.
God is very Holy.
He will judge all people.

Send Me Out

Too long in running
A life of roaming.
I finally made
A choice for Jesus.

Nobody forced me
To stop my roaming,
But Holy Spirit
Got my attention.

Holiness is the
Day to go to God.
Justified by God,
Sanctified Wholly.

Now I do study
By reading Bible,
The Bible says I
Need to be approved.

Made to worship Him,
I do this now on.
Jesus's light has shown
The way towards faith.

Wisdom is now my
Desire to get from
The Holy Bible,
Interpreting right.

I truly want to
Thank my Lord Jesus
For saving my soul.
He is my true God.

Nowhere, I will
Not go back to sin.
That life is over.
It's totally done.

Now time will begin
To tell if I do
Go back to sinning.
A test over time.

Family will see
If sinning had stopped,
The people, the Church
And Holy Father.

I say let them see.
My testimony
Will continue on
For I was saved.

Keep me in your prayers.
Pray I stand steady
Towards my Jesus
When Satan attacks.

Time is coming soon.
Lord before you come
The people need to be
Saved from Satan's Hell.

Let me go to them
Who need a Savior,
Lord Jesus Messiah
He was promised.

By poems or by praying,
Give me Your guidance
In reaching the world
Where the need is great.

Let me be the man
Whom continue to
Be acceptable,
Clean with a clear heart.

Servants of God

Father is Holy.
Jesus is the Way.
Servants shall go
To Our Father God.

Lord Jesus sent to
Us, God's servants,
The Holy Spirit to
Live in our body.

Christian needs all Three.
We are not complete
Without going to
The "One" Holy God.

The Trinity is the
Only Truth of God.
We know we've written
So much about this.

Make known whom you do
Believe our God is.
There are many gods
Trying to get us.

Wolves amongst us.
These false movements
Trying to get our
Eyes off Holy God.

Satan really knows,
This fallen angel.
How he tries to make
Himself higher god.

Now is the choosing!
"GOD" or maybe I.
Satan or small gods.
Cults and false doctrines.

Joshua was a servant.
He chose to serve God.
Not just him only,
But his family.

David was a servant.
Wrote psalms to God
And asked forgiveness.
He truly loved God.

John, the disciple,
Wrote many books.
He sat next to God
At the Last Supper.

Paul, the Apostle.
Saul saw Jesus on
The Damascus Road.
Pharisee to Christian.

Stephen followed God.
He was the first martyr.
Saul lead the stoning
Of Stephen back then.

Now God's servant Paul.
He wrote many book
Of our New Testament.
He had suffered much.

All these servants were,
Plus so many more.
Too many for this poem.
They really loved God.

How do you serve God?
We do follow Jesus
In the Holy Bible.
Do not get puffed up.

Some Good People

A worldly talker
With a worldly view
Most of the time too,
Some are good people.

They do try to be
A helper whom gives.
Many times they don't
Heal the problems now.

Many deny God
Whom they do not know.
They're knowledgeable
In their many fields.

They are called today
People who care too.
They do deny God,
No surrendering.

They believe mankind
Will solve all problems,
Yet they are empty
As to know how too.

Does mankind need God?
Problems do remain
Because they are now
Dying without God.

Only Jesus can
Help everyone.
He is the Healer
In our hurting times.

Will good people come
To a saving Lord
Who will accept them?
For now, they are lost.

Jesus, Mom, and I

I am living the Christian life
With my Jesus whom I do love.
For Mom was my example in life.
She loved Jesus with all her heart.

Jesus is the True way to go
To Our Father whom had loved us.
We received the Holy Spirit.
My mother had longed prayed for me.

I hold on to Jesus my Lord
Whom was with me in the hard times.
I am amaze by Holy God's Love
That comes to me every day.

My mom was always ready to
Give to all God's encouragements.
A relationship I saw in Her
To hold on to Jesus's Loving Hands.

A glory-filled grace demanded both
Mom and I to receive Jesus.
A faith that will only see God's Grace.
A time to accept these gifts from God.

The reason we find happiness
Is due to the Holy Bible too.
Sixty-six books all about God
To be read and to be studied.

Holy Bible collecting no dust.
My mom and I do pray together
Almost every day to Jesus.
My mother is my prayer partner.

Time as it is cannot be stopped.
Our bodies are not young anymore.
There is only one life we do live.
We had given our hearts to Jesus.

She is my mother whom knows
About reaching out to others,
For faith in Jesus begins to be
The life she wants others to see.

We shall go to our own churches
By loving the only true Jesus.
God wants to be with each person,
For we shall surrender to Him.

We move with the only True Jesus.
He came into this world to die.
Crucified, Father had sent Him. Risen,
Jesus did the third day.

There are many who need Jesus.
Father has now restored mankind.
Jesus is alive to move people
To stay away from sins today.

We did ask Jesus for forgiveness.
It is by Grace Jesus gives it.
A life Mom and I want to live
By settling our faith in Jesus.

Interpreting the Holy Bible
Literally when it needs to be
Is the correct way to read it.
God can do what He does say.

Mom knows the gospel story
Due to God's own ministry.
Born again, Mom and I are.
A life the Holy Spirit moves us.

If Mom should die before me,
There will not be sadness only.
She will be alive with Jesus then.
A new body that fails no more.

Sunday Schools

A wish Christians have
For all lost children,
Let us reach them for
Jesus while they're young.

"Read about God, child,"
Said the nice pastor. "Go to Jesus, child,"
Said the teacher too.

One day the child sees
Saved by grace, Jesus.
They heard the sermons
And teacher's lessons.

"A New Creation,"
The Bible does say.
They ask forgiveness,
and they come to God.

It is Christian's hope
That children believes,
"Maturing in Christ
Through eternity."

We praise Jesus
And say, "Thanks to God."
Another is born
In God's family.

Take Me Home

I shall go faster to God
I shall talk to sweet Jesus.
Jesus, if you desire,
Do take me home in God's time.

I am not talking about
Suicide to want heaven.
Jesus is on His own throne.
Praise and glory to God.

I have God's presence today.
Holy Father I do love.
I know through Jesus's own blood,
And His own grace am I saved.

I am sanctified wholly
I am going to heaven.
I keep myself from sinning.
Closer do I want my Jesus.

Let me faithfully obey.
The world causes each person
To choose between Lord Jesus
Or to choose Satan in life.

No one, except the savior,
Can turn a sinner into
A saint in our own travels.
It does take an open heart.

One day I had turned away
Living in strife with Jesus.
Now, looking back is painful.
I don't fall in Satan's snare.

How quickly life is moving?
If it is God's own choosing,
Do take me anytime, Lord.
Faithfully, I served Jesus.

The Bible Does Say So

True Way is God's Way
Jesus, He is the Way.
Who said only Jesus?
The Bible does say so.

Be True to Holy Word;
Jesus, He is the Word.
God/Man is Jesus Christ.
The Bible does say so.

Do know the True God's Son
Jesus, He is the Son.
The Son had come to Earth.
The Bible does say so.

Move on to True New Life
Jesus, He is the Life.
No secular living.
The Bible does say so.

Know the God of True Love
Jesus, He is the Love.
World does not love us.
The Bible does say so.

Our True God is the king;
Jesus, He is the king.
This honor comes from God.
The Bible does say so.

The True God does have light
Jesus, He is the light.
Shine says the Lord Jesus.
The Bible does say so.

Do be True to the Lord
Jesus, He is the Lord.
Rule Your people today.
The Bible does say so.

The Stormy Life

The Stormy life
All around me
Brings God to me
To calm my life

The long winter
With holidays
Can be too much
Noise in my life.

Springtime does rain,
Not hot or cold.
People moving
Back into life.

Summer sunshine
Brings in hot times.
In my moments.
Life moves onward.

Fall cools down now
The colorful trees
With leaves falling.
I'm getting older.

Onward I go
Another year
Of changing times
I do move with.

I cling to God
Until life ends
In the cycle
Of stormy life.

These Actions

Major actions, I do
Pray to my Holy God.
I am seeking God's Will
For my life I do live.

Remove my wrong actions
Where I do not see right.
There are times I do want
Something from my God.

Sudden actions are bad
When I do not think out
The consequences I had.
Was this what God wanted?

Let good actions, Jesus,
Come out of me only;
These are the examples
Christians should continue.

Other people's actions
Are normal reactions
If they are bringing up,
Or they are bringing down.

Behavior actions
Do seem to happen too,
Especially selfish.
"Believe," says the world.

Dominating actions
The world expresses
To silence the Christians
Are becoming normal.

Forgive action by those
Whom do hate the way I
Love my Savior Jesus.
Show them love always.

This Is How Life Goes

Mankind decreases.
Our God Increases.
This is how life goes.
Mankind in their place.

Mankind created.
God is Creator.
This is how life goes.
Mankind in their place.

Mankind slavery.
God is mastering.
This is how life goes.
Mankind in their place.

Mankind redeeming.
God is redeemer.
This is how life goes.
Mankind in their place.

Mankind unbelief.
God is Truthfulness.
This is how life goes.
Mankind in their place.

Mankind praying less.
God's intersession.
This is how life goes.
Mankind in their place.

Mankind commanded.
God is commanding.
This is how life goes.
Mankind in their place.

Mankind meaningless.
God is meaningful.
This is how life goes.
Mankind in their place.

To Be with Him

God of my soul
Come to me now.
It is so nice
To be with Him.

The night is dark,
Yet God does shine.
He does love me
To be with Him.

"Bless me," I say
As God does give.
He gives me gifts
To be with Him.

This night I pray
To be with God.
God does hear me
To be with Him.

God is so near
To my heart now.
I do want joy
To be with Him.

God does mold me
In what to be.
A man who wants
To be with Him.

Glad to serve God
As night goes on.
Grace is for me
To be with Him.

God, I stand on
The Word of God.
This is my way
To be with Him.

True

Do I believe
God answers prayers?
Forever true
I do believe.

I do God's Will
By obeying.
My true caring
While I do pray.

"The name above
Every name."
This true Scripture
Is so awesome.

The Word did dwell
Upon this Earth.
True Jesus Christ
Became a Man.

I do pray day,
Night, and bedtime.
These earnest prayers
To my Love, God.

The families
Need to pass on.
True salvation
Each generation

Beware, Satan
Is defeated.
A true loser
Getting the lost.

God sent Jesus
The Promised One.
Are you true to
Be a Christian?

Urgent!

I do believe people parish
When they die without God's Son
Jesus was left outside their heart,
Not accepting Him as Savior.

I saw many people trying
To find something worth living for
They turn to many religions
Since they never knew Jesus Christ.

I knew people only needed
To know about Jesus the Lord
My urgent plea is my desire
To tell the ones who die onward.

Too many reject Jesus Christ
To go into a place called hell
They did not accept Jesus
In a day they heard the warnings.

They lived a life without Jesus
And knew not God personally
Someday Jesus will deliver
All lost to the Lake of Fire.

He died, was risen, and ascended.
Jesus removed the sinner's penalty
It is God's true life's events.
We all need to go to Jesus.

Our Salvation is important
Since failure leads without our God
One God! Father, Son, and Spirit
Are here to stay forever, Amen.

Victory

Move onward people
To be delivered.
Do you have victory
Over your sinning?

Do not forget to
Talk to God in prayer.
Do let God work in
Your sinful life now.

Let Christians witness
To you about your soul.
Jesus is open
Whom does love you so.

Pray out to Jesus
For forgiveness too.
God is always next
To you in your life.

Open the Bible
And read the Gospels
About Jesus love
Whom He had died for you.

Jesus lives today;
He arose from the tomb.
God is in your life
For you asked forgiveness.

Now you are washed clean.
This is when you do
Stop sinning on.
Your life is now His.

Holy Spirit lives
Within your own soul,
For you are saved
To continue learning.

We Do Feel

This is the time to see our dreams
Upon this land we do call home
Where giving and taking runs on
Loving, hating, and desiring.

To laugh or to cry, remember.
People surrounding us today.
Events played out before God.
There shall be excuses today.

Living examples where we do
Demonstrate our kinds of actions
Played out before the Holy God.
Sins causes much more anxiety.

We do know the good and the bad
We cannot find it without God.
If we do think about ourselves,
Questions usually not found.

If we fight against all evil,
We failed if God is pushed out.
God gives wisdom to our questions
Seeking and finding His Own Way.

We stand also with Lord Jesus
Without being stained by this world.
A Christian's love is found in God.
We are blessed by knowing Jesus.

Some days we may be in valleys
There are days on the mountaintop.
We do go along with Jesus
Most eagerly keeping him close.

How do the lost come to Jesus?
Allow Holy Spirit guidance.
If we do seek our own glory,
Our own ways will be our ego.

What's the Fuss?

What is all the fuss about?
I agree, there was Jesus
Whom had so many followers.
My Bible I own sits closed.

Don't I acknowledge Jesus
I see He was somebody.
Do I really need to see
Any changes in my life?

My mother has become one.
Does this not mean anything?
I do see changes in her
Whom claims a way to God.

A Christian, I think, does want
A choice only I can make.
Let me think about this fuss.
Tomorrow, I'll need Jesus.

We ended in a prayer
To tell me I am created
To worship God of Bible.
Why tell me sin is not good?

I do basically believe
People do try to live good
If my friends do believe this,
Does Jesus fit in my needs?

They just keep on coming back,
And each time I let them talk
Maybe, I need Holy God.
He does seem stable to me.

My own life is out of Jesus,
And what they have I may also
God, are You really real today
In a life full of hopeless dreams.

Now the parable is this:
The seed is the Word of God. See Luke 11: 11, KJV.

Who Is This God Jesus Christ?

A day gone and a day lost.
Who is this God Jesus Christ?
Is He available now?
Do reach me whom is seeking.

You said, "Go to Jesus Christ."
Who is this God Jesus Christ?
Is He teaching like a God?
So far nothing satisfies.

Can I hear what you're saying?
Who is this God Jesus Christ?
Is He reliable now?
You say He died and was risen.

Now you say, "He is alive."
Who is this God Jesus Christ?
Is He understandable?
Yes, I would like to meet Him.

The book says, "Holy Bible."
Who is this God Jesus Crist?
Is He a lovable God?
Yes, He is Holy also.

Explain Christian, "What is Faith?"
Who is this God Jesus Christ?
Is He really the Savior?
Yes, I do want to have faith.

Can my sins be forgiven?
Who is this God Jesus Christ?
Is He able to save me?
Can I pray the sinner's prayer?

What do I do now Christian?
Saved by this God Jesus Christ.
Is He wanting me to grow?
Let me start reading Bible.

Why

Why did it take so long, Lord?
My understanding was lacking
Due to my wrong ideas on
How Holiness Movement worked.

Why did my reading the Bible
Make me come to Jesus sooner?
I searched the scriptures, and I
Read Holiness Writers books.

Why did it at once it had came
Together all I had been reading?
It all finally made sense because
The Holy Spirit was working on me.

Why could I finally stop sinning?
It was due to Justification when
I gave my life over to Jesus, God.
I tried it my way, and I had failed.

Why is Holiness important to God?
I am to be Holy due to Jesus being
Holy, Just, Righteous, and True.
He is the Truth I especially need.

Why is Jesus everlasting today?
He went to the cross on Friday.
He arose the third day, Sunday.
Jesus is alive forever with Father.

Why did I get so disgusted, God?
I failed so many times on my own.
I had transgressions against Jesus.
Praise God, He washed me clean.

Why is God keeping me faithful?
I love Him and wish to be Holy.
My God is the Trinity today,
Father, Son, and Holy Spirit.

Wrong Hell

"Wrong way,', says the pastor.
Hell is not the way to go.
It is a place for unsaved
People to go when they die.

"Wrong choice," says the pastor.
The choice for Jesus is gone.
You're dead and you're alive
In a place called hopeless.

"Wrong thought," says the pastor.
God shall never bargain
When you do die someday.
Guilty without the blood.

"Wrong sign," says the pastor.
The sign to hell is not fun.
You will be judge by God
Before you're cast in hell.

"Wrong hope," says the pastor.
All your wicked ways will
Not be there in hell too.
Hell is not the place for beer.

"Wrong place," says the pastor.
Peace is not found in hell.
It's a place of punishment
For not going to Jesus.

"Wrong love," says the pastor.
Love is tossed out in hell.
Alone in your agony
With no water for your tongue.

"Wrong life," says the pastor.
Hell will be no picnic.
There will be a place where
The worm will not go away.

You and I

God does know people,
And He died for them.
Christian or not one
God does love us all.

God answers His Way
By our faithful prayers.
He knows what we think
He knows our own hearts.

Sorry, God, if I failed;
The lost need Jesus.
Encouraging Word
Is to be on God.

I seek no glory
Of my own power.
God, You're my own
Way I do handle life.

If God tells me to
Do anything now,
Show me, for I am
Set in my ways, Lord.

I will tell the truth
From now on, Jesus.
I just got to be
Tactful when to tell.

Wisdom is what I
Need from Holy God.
Sometimes I feel like
I am wrong at times.

Let me get along
With all people too.
Even when they get
On my nerves, Jesus.

Made Whole

Love has shown my God does care
By the way He made me whole.
Holy God has given me
God of the Holy Bible.

I had no grasping in life.
Sin I had was about me.
What can make me so happy
Without knowing Jesus Christ?

The war that had possessed me
Within my inner feelings,
Jesus healed my own mind,
And He healed my own body.

Exposed was my own sins too
When I asked God to clean me.
Do wash God and cleanse me God.
A New Creation I am.

I ran God's race to Heaven.
No turning myself around
When I got nearer to God.
Jesus, I want to be Yours.

Either I am God's only,
Or I am Satan's only.
Middle ground does not exist.
Lukewarm Christians on hell's path.

Holiness that Jesus gives
Comes to me by Holy Ghost.
God has continued with me
My own body shall serve God.

Witnessing moves my own soul
To tell others about God.
Jesus does make people whole.
My God does reach out to all.

Merciful

My Jesus, my merciful God.
My past, I was so ugly.
A time before knowing God.
This old life, I was too bold.

A lost past, I had fought God,
Unbelieving false actions.
Sure, I did not show hatred
My ideas were not godly.

Jesus is merciful God.
God forgave my wicked past.
A separation due to sins
Caused by my depravity.

Will God have mercy on me?
This life I lived was wicked.
God, I ask for your presence.
I need more than myself now.

Merciful God do rule me.
Imagine, you gave me a
Choice to go to You, Jesus.
You knew me before my birth.

What if someday I will die.
Will mercy of God be shown?
I know I need redemption,
Grace is my only option.

I do all here for heaven.
I want to be with Jesus
This time God showed me mercy.
It's the day God takes me home.

As for now, I tell others.
He will have mercy on them.
If they live for Holy God,
They can receive a new life.

Life Lessons

Father God, do I realize
How Jesus's death brought me life.
This hope moves my memory.
There is all Truth in my God.

My faith magnifies Jesus,
Developing maturity.
I do seek understanding,
"Why Jesus became man/God?"

Why am I a believer?
God's Holy Word inspires me.
This keeps me worshipping God.
I'd love my God, or I'd die.

Wisdom comes to me by God.
He gives it to me today.
I wait quietly in prayer
To gain more wisdom from God.

Am I a righteous man?
I'm saved to be guided on.
In Jesus, I am righteous.
My righteousness comes from God.

I move with the changing times,
For I'm centered on Jesus.
God moves my very own soul
I am hungry for God's Word.

I sing a song about God.
It goes on with a rhythm.
I mostly sing alone too
Since I do not sing so good.

Life changes during my life
It brings me closer to God.
Please, God, remove the old man.
I'm to be made new and whole.

A Loving God

I love God in this poem
Receiving always the
Times he is so good and
He has been with me.

God wants me to be true
To Him whom loves me too.
I gave my life to God,
And God saved my own life.

There is a time to be
Totally with Jesus
All alone and all in
Prayer to Holy Father.

Take my life in God's hands
I place my faith to You.
You are the author of
All I worship in Thee.

Tonight I want to tell
The world about Your Love.
Love too amazing God.
A hope for my own peace.

Help me to understand
The Bible passages
Speaking to my own heart.
You're always on my mind.

You are so near to me
I just want to worship
And to adore you too.
It's easy to Love Jesus.

What should I do, Jesus?
You gave me Your Own Love.
Obedience is what
You do want from me.

I trust Holy Father
With all of my own life
With all of my devotion
I am now so complete.

A long time in the past
I ran away from God.
Now I run to Jesus
As fast as I can move.

My walk and my talk is
Improving as time moves.
Closer to God I do want
Until I am in my grave.

My soul shall continue
Praising everything
God made in His Kingdom
In heaven up above.

The Holy Spirit knows
My own heart, Help me!
He is in my own dreams
Even when I am sleeping.

I like to be going
To Church with people
Of like mind towards God.
He is so near to me.

I do have time to talk
With what is on my mind
Everything to God.
He is my stability.

He keeps my sanity
In a messed-up world.
I can survive the days
By total submission.

A Process God Does Care

We believe God is the Way,
Yet Christians may know God
When we get Justified.
A process God does care.

We believe God is Holy,
Yet Christians can be Holy
When we do get Sanctified.
A process God does care.

We believe God is Perfect,
Yet Christians can be perfect.
Jesus is our example.
A process God does care.

We believe God does Serve,
Yet Christians may serve too,
Christian ministries now.
A process God does care.

We believe God Knows All,
Yet Christians has the Bible.
Scriptures do speak to us.
A process God does care.

We believe God does Hear,
Yet Christians do also hear
From God while we do pray.
A process God does care.

We Believe God has wisdom,
Yet Christians ask for wisdom
When we walk with Jesus.
A process God does care.

We believe God is One God,
Yet Christians sees Trinity,
Father, Son, and Holy Spirit.
A process God does care.

Accused

Losing accused,
It was a Friday.
People had done
What High Priest want.

Standing accused,
Lies made by men
Whom their stories
Did not tell truth.

Staying accused,
He saw Pilate.
All said and done,
Pilate washed hands.

Hurting accused,
Spit upon Him.
Hit Him with hands,
Crown Him with thorns.

Whipping accused,
Bloody accused.
He had let them
Hatefully do.

Walking accused,
Carry the cross.
Bleeding on it,
Unwanted man.

To take Him down.

Nailing accused,
Agony too.
Why we put God
To death that day?

Hanging Accused,
Forgiving crowd.
Saving a crook
On His right side.

Watching accused,
Dying on cross.
Cursing people
Brutal attack.
Dying accused,
Spear in side.
Water and blood
Came out His side.

Taking accused,
The empty tomb
Where He stayed
Sealed by Rome.

Being accused
He did no wrong.
Lamb who died for
The people sins

Seeing accused,
All hope was gone
On wooden Cross
Disciples ran

Willing accused,
Forgiving them.
Obedient
To the Father.

Knowing accused,
Not ordering
The angels then
To take Him down

Winning accused,
He took the shame.
He knew what He
Was doing then.

Hating accused,
He knew how He
Will be handled
By the world.

Giving accused,
Dead and buried
No way out then.
All hope was lost

After Altar Call

After altar call, where I do begin?
I got to tell about Jesus my Lord.
A Christian so hungry and so ready,
I had given my life to Jesus Christ.

This was me many years ago at church.
A new babe in Christ ready to go out
And tell all people whom given me life
A new meaning and a new direction.

Everything surrounding my own life,
I wished I knew the Holy Bible more.
Reading every chance I was given
Spare time, I got out my Holy Bible.

My interpretation at beginning lacked
A full understanding of the Scriptures.
What I did not know, I made up with zeal
Quoting passages for the first time then.

I had lived in darkness for just too long.
Now there is something new giving me hope
On becoming a person who is saved.
Meaning was lacking, yet I study on.

The discipline as a young new Christian
Lacked for I was in the military service.
This was a time I had gone to services.
These messages all I done was listen.

There were some misunderstandings along
The ways of learning about Christianity.
I had wanted to express what I learned.
Sometimes it was some concepts offtrack.

These early military years after my call
To the need to tell what I learned
I wanted to change our societies' ills.
I spoke out where I thought was wrong.

I had slowly learned to keep my mouth shut
At the times I should listen and not talk.
I was so happy to hear the pastors
Preaching a message I saw was for me.

Gospel intake was my happiness then.
The one I most needed others speak on
What the Holy Trinity really does mean?
This is the God I knew was biblical.

My own desires centered on Bible
And what it had to saw with what I heard.
My own zeal drove many people to see
That I do need to be a little calmer.

My moving almost every two years,
There was no one ready to disciple.
This didn't stop me going to services
Every chance I had got to go to.

In my early years, I would shake their hands
Pastors of any church, I was so happy.
I was so hungry for God's Word back then.
My shift work kept me away just so much.

God's Word in my own processing Bible
Was really done on my own time frame,
Yet the pastors explained so well the truth
That I heard making me look deeper in Bible.

Altar Call

Only Way is the narrow road leading to Father,
Yet the way on the wide road continues towards Hell.
There is now salvation through the Son, Jesus Christ.
The World is saturated on the godless path.

It does take the Gospel road leading to Jesus.
We shall give our heart and soul to the Son of God.
Yes, the Holy Spirit whom Christians do listen to
Does tell everyone the Holy Bible is True.

Christians love Holy God; the trinity is true.
Unsaved have no concept on whom Father God is.
Why do the lost go unawares down a wide path?
Why do they believe they know the Holy Father?

The unbeliever believes in goodness today.
They think this depravity we have tipped the scale.
Really, only good works does not save anyone.
The Holy Bible is very clear to understand.

The Lord leads the redeemed. The lost always searching.
A true life with Jesus shows a God who does care.
This darkness of the lost souls continues onward.
We acknowledge only to Jesus about our own sins.

Do take the step of asking Jesus to forgive.
This is leading many lost to see the cruel cross.
Jesus whom had bled His own blood so painfully.
This was the day Jesus took our sins on Himself.

Don't forget the Resurrection of our dear Lord.
It was three days after Jesus Crucifixion.
Do understand the importance of this truth now.
Forever, the Lord Jesus shall rule His Kingdom.

The altar call within the Church Sanctuary
Is seeking God's presence into our empty lives.
In the sanctuary, Christians are praying for
Them whom live in darkness comes into the True Light.

Another Day

Either they are not happy
Or they think they are happy.
They are focused on something
Worth their lives to follow.

When time do changes on,
Life has many inner thoughts.
There is nowhere to get too.
Once they are there, life changes.

Cross out another day, also.
Times moves while we do nothing.
Goals arrives, it goes away
As fast as living does come.

Who does inspire us also,
Famous athletic coach,
Lawyer after many years,
Or having a family?

What thoughts are you having?
Are we not a moody people?
Sometimes it can be love,
Or sometimes hate comes along.

So many attitudes, God,
On who you are or are not.
Who really are these gods?
One who the book tells you.

Is there no greater test?
A test who tells who God is.
Christians have Holy Bible.
It has no errors in it.

World religions are not tried
For their own accuracies.
Does their book have a true god?
Holy Bible stands life's test.

Atheists are amongst us.
They believe Darwin's Theory.
Theory is not a true law
They have no proof nowadays.

Science nowadays doesn't know.
Evolution is a joke.
It requires more faith than
Creation any time of day.

Only humans do abort
As a means of birth control.
A death of a baby is
Not just tissue lifeless.

Life without Jesus is harsh.
Sins do grip at our own soul.
This is why people are
Looking for something lasting.

I do not condemn you.
It is only Jesus who
Gives people another chance.
He gave mankind the Holy Bible.

Father God loves people too.
Jesus redeemed our lives.
Sins are removed by the blood
Of Jesus when took our sins.

Become a Christian today.
A multitude of sinning
Are cleansed away when we do
Accept Jesus Savior God.

Jesus is the savior of mankind
Of whom Jesus lives forever.
Only He can forgive sins
That the saved do give up.

Atheist

"Where's Your God," says the atheist,
And proud of his intellect.
A smugness of his World to
Be a superior mankind.

A mind-set wanting no God
Mocking at this Holy God.
Atheists will go to meetings
And find a cause to fight on.

They do speak their blasphemies.
Ignorant of the Bible,
They want to rule all mankind.
Many laws against Christians.

In their minds, we're enemies
There is no God anywhere.
Christians do believe in myths
That Jesus is also God.

They fight the Christians in court
To separate us from going
Out to witness to lost souls,
Dangerous to the country.

Constitution must now change
Because they want to stop us.
Christians shall not be stopped now
From witnessing to the lost.

If we are to be punished
By our society today,
God will be first in our lives,
Even if we are martyred now.

Christianity is no game
In a World full of hatreds.
Why do you intolerant
Atheist live to hate us?

Boldness

Boldly wipe away your tears
As loved ones gone unto God.
Follow on with your beliefs.
We will be with them someday.

Boldly face people's hatreds
Against the Lord you do serve.
Jesus is our example
Whom had accepted the Cross.

Boldly stop all your sinning.
This act does keep you unsaved.
God cannot look upon sin
God will not accept any.

Boldly seek for lost sinners.
Let people know about God.
He is the one called Jesus.
Jesus whom speaks so boldly.

Boldly find the True Faith.
Apostles found the True Way
To a God whom they worshipped.
They had many hardships then.

Boldly find the peace God gives.
Peace only in Jesus Christ.
Have the power God commands
To face peace in your turmoil.

Boldly take the narrow way
That leads us to God's heaven.
Living a sinless lifestyle.
We go onto Jesus's path.

Boldly get taught with Jesus.
Holy Spirit moves my soul
To always go to my Lord,
Savior, Redeemer, and God.

Boldly shout when you sing on
With an amen occasionally.
Show others, especially
They lost the Joy God gives us.

Boldly love the unlovely.
Act upon your own heartfelt
Friendship by taking them to
The church that preaches Jesus.

Boldly trust Holy Bible.
It is always showing us
Why we do keep Holiness.
This is very important.

Boldly speak about Jesus
Who is the Way to Father.
At the time we ask Jesus,
We get the Holy Spirit.

Boldly grasp unto Jesus
When your life seems so empty.
Jesus will fill all today
To keep us in fellowship.

Boldly pray God's Word today.
Make us to know how today.
We do believe God does it all.
We ask in faith we do seek.

Boldly train up your children
To give their heart to Jesus.
Let them show how they do love.
May they grow and stay with God.

Boldly sow the seeds today.
We will live to show Jesus.
Believing the lost will see
The way to Holy Father God.

Changed

Not worst, just better.
A life with Jesus.
It is easier
To handle problems.

Now saved, I have God.
A relationship.
My love for Jesus
Grows even stronger.

I've found, I leave not.
I am a Christian.
No going today
After my old life.

My past, forgiven.
With Jesus's own blood
And the Grace of God,
Now God lives in me.

This race, a journey.
Jesus, I stay on track.
I go with a pace
Onward to heaven.

Bible, Word of God.
He fills the pages
Of all He has done.
I read, memorize.

God's love, I received.
I love Him so much.
He is on my mind
Always, forever.

True Peace, Jesus gives.
Christian forever.
I will handle life
With the Peace of God.

Christian Thoughts

Christian behavior
Seen within Christians
Needs to be shown now.
We are witnesses.

Our Holy Father
Sent mankind Jesus
Whom went to the Cross
At Calvary's Tree.

God shall be lifted up
Before the World.
Christians shine your light
Where there is darkness.

Satan does deceive
Sometimes the elect.
These worldly acts
Are stumbling blocks.

Are we Sanctified
Wholly before God?
Making disciples
Being Spirit filled.

Can Christians please all?
This we cannot do.
Satan does attack
The nonbeliever.

Hatred continues
Within our own lands.
Martyr's continues,
Open hostilities.

Death in many lands,
Possibility.
In our own country
We hold on to God.

Decisions are made
After our own prayers.
God does move this way.
All times, be ready.

What will be lasting?
Heaven is our goal.
Christians knows this as
Glorification.

Christians are hungry
For Jesus's return.
Are you now watching
And prepared for Him.

Are we to obey?
We know God's Own Way.
God will tell us all
"Well done" or depart.

I shall pray to God
Whom I love so much.
My own soul does yearn
To do all God says.

Are Christians tested
In our own conflicts?
God made a way for
Us to handle life.

What is a true must.
We choose to follow
Our God above all,
Both men and women.

Should Christians believe
Jew's are God's people.
The Holy Bible
Does say this is true.

Come to God

Keep me to the end.
Salvation is lost
If I do sin on.
Stay true to Jesus.

You may say how so.
A person who sins
Due to hardened heart
Will not confess sin.

If they do confess
Sinning all the time
For repeated sins,
You need to stop it.

Continue sinning
Will send you to hell.
Do not think you can
Believe any less.

Christians need to go
All the way with God.
Do not fall away
At the end of life.

Hold on to Jesus
Living by His Grace.
God cannot look at
Sin due to His Word.

The Bible is true.
People are to be
Obedient to
A Holy Just God.

Sanctified wholly,
God does want people
Not to stop only
At Justification.

Grow into Jesus
As your example
On how to live a
Life of Holiness.

Take a stand people
To say you obey
What Jesus does in
The Holy Bible.

I know there is a
God speaking the truth
Due to my reading
And praying to God.

I do talk to God.
My desires are
To be all ready
To listen also.

You say I'm crazy!
If talking to God
Makes me so crazy,
I guess so be it.

I say they are wrong.
The Bible is the
Truth we all do need
To be guided by.

From faith in God,
This is what I want
Is not to sin on,
And to be His child.

The Holy Bible
shall be presented
To the lost people
As I talk to them.

Decide

Decide to stay the course
Truer to God my Lord.
I do look at myself
If God wants any change.

Decide to be more than
Just doing lip service.
I will use what I learn
For the glory of God.

Decide to believe on
The Word of Holy God.
I want to be like Him
In all that I will do.

Decide to love only God,
Total surrendering.
I depend on Jesus
By giving Him my all.

Decide to be reminded
Daily what God has done.
He went to Calvary.
God does love me so much.

Decide to speak about
The goodness of Jesus.
I see God is Holy
And does love me also.

Decide to stand today
Against willful sinning.
I will be a person
Choosing not to sin on.

Decide to speak the truth
That lies upon my heart.
White lies are still lies
Still after I say it.

Decide to use Scriptures
In all the days of life.
I do want to know what
The words of Bible says.

Decide to run the race
Paul had talked about.
I will not stop my race
Until I cross the line.

Decide to do the good
Fight God wants us to do.
I will do what is right
And seek His will for me.

Decide to reach out to
The lost lonely people.
I was once without hope,
Yet I found my Savior.

Decide to bring in hope
To a lost dying world.
I want to be the one
Who says, "Send me, Jesus."

Decide to take up Cross
And to do what God wants.
I gladly bare the Cross
Of Calvary this day.

Decide to keep up peace
With people who love God.
I know differences
Need working out today.

Decide to listen to
Jesus within our lives.
I want to hear from God
And to be in awe too.

Draw Me Closer, Jesus

Draw me closer, Jesus
Daily in my prayers
I'll do as You tell me.
Help me to grasp it all.

Draw me closer, Jesus
As I witness to each
Person in my own life.
Do go to Jesus Christ.

Draw me closer, Jesus
Loving You with my heart
And with my own life,
God, I want Jesus today.

Draw me closer, Jesus
Does come from You only.
My Jesus is the Word
That became a Man/God.

Draw me closer, Jesus,
For I do feel tired.
It is true that God does
Strengthen me to go on.

Draw me closer, Jesus
Whom Justified me to
Be Wholly Sanctified
As I do mature on.

Draw me closer, Jesus
By my faith in my God.
A free gift, I receive
Grace and with no works.

Draw me closer, Jesus
The Holy Spirit moves
Me by reminding me
It is Jesus I go to.

Face God

"Face the fact of our God."
What will the people do?
No one knows until God
Reveals the True Jesus.

"Face the life of our God."
What must we do, Jesus?
Jesus told us the truth
By the way he had lived.

"Face the past of our God."
What must the Messiah do?
The Holy Bible shows
Scripture prophecies True.

"Face the marks of our God."
What does Calvary do?
Death did come to our Lord,
And very cruelly done.

"Face the day of our God."
What does Jesus then do?
He had risen that day
The tomb could not keep Him.

"Face the light of our God."
What does the light shall do?
Light will show through darkness
Jesus is the True Light.

"Face the names of our God."
What does all His names do?
The Trinity does show
All the different names.

"Face the Grace of our God."
What does Grace have to do?
We learn that mankind work,
Just cannot save any.

Fallen Away

Pray for the fallen.
They knew Jesus Christ.
They belong to God,
Yet they fell away.

They had God's Spirit.
He was in their lives,
Yet they walked away.
Sins remain in them.

Will they return to
The Lord repenting?
They had lost their ways.
Bible says, "First Love."

A person can lose
Their salvation too.
Those who disagree,
But what does God say?

The Holy Bible
Does have the Scriptures
Supporting that they
Freely walked away.

We say this to be
Not judgmental.
Only God does judge.
He does know their heart.

Satan can get a
Person deceived too.
Their faith in Jesus
Left under hardships.

Times get very hard,
Or they do not want
What the Gospel says.
They ignore Scriptures.

These examples are
Off top of my head.
Yet I believe they
Will prove people leave.

Some say a person
Was never saved
If they do leave God.
Let's look in the Bible.

Lord, open our eyes
To God's Holy Truth.
Sin separates us
From a Holy God.

Take the Far Country.
The son wasted life.
He returned back
To the Father God.

Take the Ten Talents.
One became lost then.
She searched for it.
Rejoiced when she found.

There were two people
While Paul was in jail
In the city, Rome.
They had also fallen.

Was it Judas who kissed
Jesus on the cheek?
He followed Jesus
Then he hung himself.

Sin, when saved or not,
God cannot look at.
Totally give your
Lives over to God.

Follow a Path

Tell me a path you follow.
I will see just who you are.
A Christian or lost person.
Death, it really does matter.

All people believe something.
Is there a god you worship?
The choices of many gods
Will lead down a wider path.

This path of light leads to God
The road is narrow, people.
This dark path leads to Satan
The road is wider, people.

The desires on this land
Brings to mankind many sins.
The sins of the people are
Written in the Holy Word.

The True Way goes to Father.
This path does give us our faith,
Our Grace and the Blood of Christ.
Please pray to the Savior God.

Make straight your path to heaven.
No detouring is allowed.
Worship the Lord with power
Of the True Holy Spirit.

The wrong wide path leads to death.
Spiritual death of our soul.
Our soul will live forever
In a place Christians call hell.

Accept Jesus as Savior.
Ask God to forgive your sins.
Accept salvation today.
Then you are on narrow path.

God Delivered Me

On a shiny day
Not too long ago,
I did not let
Go of my sins.

Burdened, I was
With so much sin.
Done outwardly
Every day.

I hated to sin.
I was depressed
For I had no
Willpower to stop.

Now I decided
I really needed
To make a choice
Once and for all.

I had God's help.
I made my choice
To stop sinning.
I knew God answered.

It's been ten weeks
I have not sinned.
Praise Jesus Christ.
He delivered me.

I do feel God's
Holy Spirit.
He gives me joy
To worship Jesus.

No turning back
To my old ways.
Straight on the road
That is narrow.

God Is My Life

Just obey Jesus
On this blessed day.
It feels like heaven,
For God is so near.

He lifts my sorrows
Off of my own hurts.
He does show me love
On my lonely days.

Never will He leave
The burdens I have.
Jesus is near me
With the open Word.

My life is so good,
For God is so near.
I pass the time too,
Prayers and praises.

My time with Jesus
Is very awesome
Because He's special
On His Truthful ways.

As I get older
And I get wiser,
It is due to God
In my life always.

People, I do pray
For your salvation.
Get rid of old life
Get hold on new life.

Christians, do get real
To a listening God.
God sees my actions
God hears my questions.

God Today

Lead me, God, today.
Holy Spirit does
Live in my own soul.
He tells me to come.

Tell me, God, today.
Jesus is God of
The Holy Bible.
It does speak to me.

Form me, God today.
You mold me in a
Loving and kind way.
Shape me always, God.

Seek me, God, today.
You are so near now.
I do fall away.
Your Word I do hear.

Teach me, God, today.
I am truly Yours
To show me the Way.
This makes me happy.

Found me, God, today.
Long time ago,
I was very lost.
Now I am all Yours.

Reach me, God today.
Life can be far
Away when I stray.
I want You, Jesus.

Love me, God, today.
You are so Holy
That I am amazed.
Let me show others.

God's Company

Faith over time does grow
By getting to know God.
The more time with Jesus
Greater our faith may be.

Interpreting correctly,
The Holy Spirit does touch
The real meaning of Scripture.
It is a time of molding.

Do not go through the motion
Of taking spiritual things
Lightly in your own life.
Meditate on God's Word.

Thank God for another day.
A time to share true faith
In a Good God and Savior.
One whom shall stay with us.

Praise to a Holy God
One whom we do receive
Each time we pray and sing.
Glory to the One True God.

Jesus, You keep us happy.
Your mercy and forgiveness
Brings completeness to life.
A soul submitted to God.

Times with God gives to us hope.
Your company's important.
If we do go our own way,
Shortly we mess things up.

Go ahead and talk to God.
We will find a listener.
At the time He does speak,
We do need to be quiet.

Welcome God into your heart.
God will fellowship then.
He will never forces us
Until we are ready.

Take time now to be saved
By a God whom is open.
Receive the Holy Spirit
When we give our hearts.

Christlike in our actions
By showing others God.
If we see a sufferer
For Jesus, do help them.

Holy Bible reading
Is our devotion to God.
We take time each day to read
About God's Mighty Works.

God made mankind from dust
He does do miracles today.
We do know He moves today
People who knows Jesus Christ.

Lord, our minds cannot find
An ending to this poem.
We will just say it is
Good in God's Company.

God's Plans

Now is the day to plan for the future.
What kingdom does not seek their goals
Of going into a battle during their planning?
God is giving Himself for our future plans.

Let Lord Jesus move our spirit in our soul.
Allow God's plans to be centered on His Will.
Do not be complacent all around ourselves.
Move to Holy God's Bible for directions.

If we do not get the plans we do want,
God does see more than we see and do.
God is the mover of all of mankind, and
We know we need God more than this World.

If we do our plans in our own desires,
We get all we deserve in the end of Life.
No one can blame God if we are in ourselves.
If we do follow Holy God, He will do for us.

If you do not read the Holy Bible ever,
Why do people curse this life is so unfair?
God does bring to all the people peace
When we do receive Jesus into our lives.

His plans are God's way for us to be His
Workmen whom will always do God's will.
His plans produce faith when it is from God.
God will never change His Holiness Way.

Believe God's Holiness to see God's Handiwork.
We do obey, and we do receive God's will.
Holy Bible reading people will grasp God
Due to the Holy Spirit living in our bodies.

Jesus, our Lord and our Savior, forevermore.
We are not the same after receiving Jesus.
Our souls do belong to His own hand's shaping.
Obedience to God requires our total surrender.

Gospel Wagon

Gospel wagon is
Where we say goodbye
To this sinful world.
Get on the wagon.

Pass on open fields
Gospel wagon goes
Where people do go.
Get on the wagon.

Through inner cities
Gospel wagon moves
Sinners to come in.
Get on the wagon.

Go up to people
In gospel wagon
For all to come in.
Get on the wagon.

Pass on the roads
With gospel wagon
Where many travel.
Get on the wagon.

Pass the worldly ones
In the gospel wagon
Showing Jesus too.
Get on the wagon.

Preachers preach on
The gospel wagon
Wherever it goes.
Get on the wagon.

Jesus is on the
Old gospel wagon
From the Holy Bible.
Get on the wagon.

Grace Only

More God, less me.
My love for God
Is what makes me
Worship Jesus.

God's forever
I'm forever.
Where will I be
After judgment.

The Book of Life
Mentioned in the
Holy Bible
Is what I know.

By "Grace Only"
Without working
My own way in
Is God's own Way.

God's Grace is not
Sinning actions,
But a desire
To stop it now.

Sinning against
God's Holiness
Is transgression
Against Jesus.

Forgiveness comes
From the Father
Through Jesus Christ
When we ask God.

Holy Jesus
Thank you today
For salvation,
Justified now.

Forgive me God,
I know I did
Wrong's against you.
I will not sin.

Hand over to God
My life of not
Easy beliefism.
Help me to stop.

Sanctify me
Lord Jesus Christ,
Savior and King.
Help me today.

I am amazed
by the many
People who are
Against Jesus.

Jesus is now
Knocking on door
Of people's hearts.
Please sup with Him.

Grace continues
To be always
Free from Jesus.
I have faith.

Jesus's own blood
Cleanses me now
Grace is the
Way to Jesus.

For God cannot
Look at our sin.
This is why
God's blood used.

He Is My Example

I pray lovingly, God.
He showed me Love.
For God is Love.
He is my example.

I pray openly, God.
He showed me Himself,
For God is open.
He is my example.

I pray for justice, God.
He showed me Justice,
For God is Just.
He is my example.

I pray merciful, God.
He showed me Mercy,
For God is Merciful.
He is my example.

I pray hopefully, God.
He showed me Hope,
For God is Hope.
He is my example.

I pray truthfully, God.
He showed me Truth,
For God is Truth.
He is my example.

I pray holiness, God.
He showed me Holy,
For God is Holy.
He is my example.

I pray nowadays, God.
He showed me today,
For God is today.
He is my example.

His Plan

Can Love of God be seen?
The Father, Creator.
His plan continues on.
Mankind needs redemption.

One Father in Heaven.
Jesus is preparing
His plan for True Christians.
Do worship Holy God?

Forever Created
By Almighty God.
His plan is so simple.
God wants our fellowship.

One Father and Master.
Jesus Cross does show us
His plan to save mankind.
God the Father does Love.

Where is this Jesus Christ?
He does live in no tomb.
His plan, He is risen.
Now I can pray to God.

Jesus is the real Son.
He's equal to Father.
His plan does never stop.
Holy Spirit shows us.

Holy Bible is Truth.
Read and do understand
His plan does show Jesus.
Jesus came for the lost.

Holy Spirit moves us.
At Pentecost, God came.
His plan to worship God.
How can I tell it all?

How Do the Lost Surrender?

How do the lost surrender?
Our acts do defy Jesus.
The World has their enticements.
In time, there is no caution.

How do the lost surrender?
Many do continue life
With Satan's own deception.
There is only one True God.

How do the lost surrender?
As ups and downs continue,
It can harden our memories
Of a wicked lonely life.

How do the lost surrender?
Time is sometimes merciless.
Death is in society.
No answers on our aging.

How do the lost surrender?
With open invitation,
Christians are witnessing on
To the lost masses, Jesus.

How do the lost surrender?
Holy Spirit does show us
The Father's Crucified Son.
Let the Love continue on.

How do the lost surrender?
Our works will not save ourselves.
Jesus had shed His own blood
Jesus's Grace can be our grace.

How do the lost surrender?
It is between God and you.
Decisions to follow God
Comes by our own surrender.

I Asked

One day, I did ask,
"Keep me faithful, God."
Life is truly filled
With many problem,

Why are problems here
Before me today?
God, only You can
Give me a true peace.

What do I live for?
Holy Spirit keeps
Jesus before me.
Get rid of old man.

Can I believe, God?
Yes, He will never
Change from day to day.
He does not have sins.

Will my transgressions
Be known unto God?
God does take away
Sins by His own blood.

Why second chances?
Did I not do it
Willingly today
To go out and sin?

Where do I start, God?
I prayed onwards
To be used by God.
Nobody forced me.

Does grace keep moving
To me a sinner.
My relationship, God,
Is to be with You.

I Feel a Bit Cold

The snowy day felt cold
I am staying in.
Like my own feelings,
I feel a bit cold.

My actions do say
To calm down today.
Like my own feelings,
I feel a bit cold.

My own pride was hurt
I need to forgive.
Like my own feelings,
I feel a bit cold.

If I do forgive,
They'll say I'm weak.
Like my own feelings,
I feel a bit cold.

Should I go to them
With my bit coldness.
Like my own feelings,
I feel a bit cold.

Lord, I have sinned
Should I call them now.
Like my own feelings,
I feel a bit cold.

No, I guess I go,
Yet it's cold outside.
Like my own feelings,
I feel a bit cold.

I have forgiven them
By going to them.
Like my own feelings,
I feel better now.

I Want More, Jesus

I want more, Jesus
Holiness today.
He is my way to
Be more holy too.

I want more, Jesus
He is my Savior,
For no one's worthy,
Except Jesus Christ.

I want more, Jesus
The Peace You give me
It drives me to You.
Nobody else will.

I want more, Jesus
I shall continue.
I worship Jesus
Each day of my life.

I want more, Jesus
I do come to You.
Sins drove me away,
But You washed me clean.

I want more, Jesus
You gave me Your Love.
How I love God so?
I will tell Him too.

I want more, Jesus
You showed grace to me.
My works will not do
That will balance scale.

I want more, Jesus
I will run onward
To finish with Jesus,
Never looking back.

In the Holy Bible

Father God, thank you
For I do go through Jesus.
I do praise and worship
The one who gave Jesus.

In the Holy Bible,
It has all I do need.
The Word of God moves.
I now know Holy God.

God came to the writers
Who are inspired to
Write under the Spirit's
Directions long ago.

Jesus fulfilled prophecy.
Both the Old and the New
Testaments told of God.
This God is Jesus Christ.

Who is the Messiah?
He is the foretold one
Coming in His own time.
It is Lord Jesus Christ.

Jesus is the center
Of what Bible's about.
There is no other one.
Have faith in Lord Jesus.

Inside of my body
Is the Holy Spirit.
He does move me to
The scriptures of the Bible.

Love was the reason for
Father had sent Jesus.
This allow the Christians
To have His fellowship.

Is This Your Question?

Who is in command?
No one but yourself
Can answer this one.
Is this your question?

Whom shall be the ruler?
Satan or Jesus?
Only two choices.
Is this your question?

How will you live life?
From the Bible,
Or in yourself now.
Is this your question?

Whom do you stand on?
Jesus as Savior,
Or Satan in hell.
Is this your question?

Do you hesitate?
A final decision
You may choose wrongly.
Is this your question?

Why am I in a rush?
I am in no way
In a hurry state.
Is this your question?

Why don't I move on?
If Jesus rule I,
I cannot have fun.
Is this your question?

Do I start sooner?
Life is not certain
In a world where Satan rules.
Is this your question?

If I go to hell,
Will I see my friends?
We had happy times.
Is this your question?

If I go to heaven,
What is there for me?
My friends are rowdy.
Is this your question?

Can I measure up?
I do like to sin.
I cannot change this.
Is this your question?

Can I work it in?
Time is too fast now.
Maybe Sunday do.
Is this your question?

What shall my friends think?
I lost my thinking
When I went to church.
Is this your question?

What's in it for me?
Can I get something
For nothing to do.
Is this your question?

Why does Christians think
The way they do things?
Lifestyle may change now.
Is this your question?

Where will this take me?
What am I to think?
I will think on this.
Is this your question?

Jesus Is All There

Faithfully, faith is required.
The multitude worship,
And they are Spirit filled.
Christian people pray on.

Tearfully, tears do come
To many on the journey.
We are heading to God's
Glorious heaven now.

Hopefully, hope to hear
Our God who is around
Today and forever.
We will thank and praise.

Wishfully, wish for grace.
It is to accept our God.
It is only in Jesus
Who will give to all.

Prayerfully, pray to God
To accept His Own Gift.
Know the way to Holy God.
Surrender all to Jesus.

Watchfully, watch for God.
His return is Christian's dreams
Of when He comes for us.
Be ready on going up.

Fearfully, fear sinning on.
God will judge all sinners.
Fear can also mean awe.
He is mighty and awesome.

Cheerfully, cheer True God.
Lift up your hand to thank.
Get happy for Jesus.
Know the joy we do have.

Jesus Is with Me

I want to show that I grew
As a good example
Of a true believer.
Jesus is with me.

I received God's grace
Truly forever
As a growing Christian.
Jesus is with me.

I believe God's blood is
From my own Savior
Jesus whom washed me clean.
Jesus is with me.

I will not fall back
To my old lifestyle
My eyes stayed on Jesus.
Jesus is with me.

I shall not sin onward,
For I had surrender
To Jesus my Lord.
Jesus is with me.

I lift up Jesus Christ
In my prayers I have
Every day I live.
Jesus is with me.

I give my all to God
By holding on to the
Word of God written.
Jesus is with me.

I love Jesus Christ
Because He had loved me
By going to the cross.
Jesus is with me.

I have faith in Jesus
Rising from the tomb
After crucifixion.
Jesus is with me.

Money

More money for me.
Society don't
Deny me from it.
Entitled to it.

Illegal migrants.
All they do hear now
About United
States of America.

Inflation rampant.
Just print more up now.
I got to have it.
It's got to be mine.

Government give it,
Immediately.
With my addictions,
I got to have it.

Work, what do you mean?
There is more money
To not work than to
Work minimum wage.

I play the scratch off.
May today I hit
Really big money,
One hundred dollars.

I go to my church
For the pie in sky.
I am so needy
I am dependent.

I desire it.
Money comes to me.
Do give it my god,
Immediately.

My God Inspires

The words come to me
From my own thinking.
I try to write poems
God wants me to give.

Poetry moves me
To open my thoughts
To other people
To know my Jesus.

Over time, I pray for
These poems to move lost
People to come to
To know my Jesus.

To talk with Jesus
Is my heart's desire
To lift up Jesus.
Jesus moves my soul.

Maturing onward
In my own writing,
I do surrender
All to Holy God.

God gave me the words
It is my own choice
To turn my writing
Over to Jesus Christ.

Poetry is for
People to read
About this Christian
Own faith in Jesus.

The writing, I pray,
Will keep on coming
To glorify God
Whom is to be praised.

My Soul's Safe with God

Live to be with God
Even when danger
Stands all around me.
My soul safe with God.

Death when it happens,
We do God's leading
Of reaching people.
My soul safe with God.

Dream on I do, God.
I serve according
To my Jesus's Will.
My soul's safe with God.

Talk to my Jesus
Every day now.
My prayers go on.
My soul's safe with God.

Peace I get from God
Because Jesus lives.
He calms my own life.
My soul's safe with God.

Strength comes from God
When I feel so weak.
He uses me sometimes.
My soul's safe with God.

Grace Jesus does give
To my very life.
I do accept it.
My soul's safe with God.

Blood in Crucifixion.
Jesus had gone through.
He really loved me.
My soul's safe with God.

Noise

Thank You for giving to me
Peace in turmoil darkness.
Days are turning to end-times
I do not know what is next.

Personally I want to
Worship the Lord even more,
Praise until the time of His
Return and thank God daily.

There are ideas on knowing
On which areas I do seek
In always doing God's Will.
I just cling unto Jesus.

Never going to my old
Ways before I was saved.
These were days of no living.
I really wasted my life.

There seems to be so much noise
In the life of finding quiet.
Peace comes from Jesus Christ.
Thanks Lord for my time with You.

Help me to be understood.
Keep me in Your Holy Love
I do not want to keep a
Fight going without peace.

Let me live in these end-times
Together with Your guidance,
For I have a goal to go
To heaven where there is no noise.

Thanks again for Your own Rule
It's not loving the world,
Especially when I see wrong.
Father, I do love Jesus.

Not in Jesus

No hatred in Jesus!
No cruelness ever.
He is a loving God
Whom died for you and I.

No loser in Jesus!
The tomb was open.
Have I become loser
By denying Jesus?

No blaspheme in Jesus!
Holy and just is Jesus.
This is my desire
To become more like Jesus.

No whimper in Jesus!
Jesus isn't a weak man.
Jesus in my weakness
Gives me His Own Strength.

No whiner is Jesus!
Jesus is a bold God.
I may wimp in my life,
Yet God gave His Power.

No darkness in Jesus!
God's light does shine onward.
Darkness may get me down,
Yet God's light picks me up.

No failing in Jesus!
Jesus knows all He does.
I do fail in my life,
But God's Son never fails.

No untruth in Jesus!
Truth does come from Jesus.
I have been untruthful,
But Jesus changed my life.

No demon in Jesus!
The Word had become flesh.
Jesus is not controlled,
For He is God today.

No disgust in Jesus!
I shall witness to all.
Tell the world Jesus is
To be lifted up now.

No lying in Jesus!
Satan is a liar.
Lord Jesus is a
Sinless God forever.

No loss in Jesus!
Satan was happy when
Jesus hung on the Cross,
Third day Resurrection.

No faithless in Jesus!
Jesus did what He said.
Holy Bible says so.
Do not deny the Truth.

No sickness in Jesus!
He healed the lame and blind.
I know Jesus had told
Many times not to sin.

No wicked in Jesus!
He is pure without spot.
The Incarnate Jesus
Will be a good God.

No deceit in Jesus!
There is no hidden life.
Faithful to the Father
By coming to mankind.

Oh! So Foolish

Where is old man?
Oh! So foolish.
The sins we have
Do lead to hell.

Why believe it?
Oh! So foolish.
You do say that
There is no God.

Why do you laugh?
Oh! So foolish.
Hell is a place
Of endless pain.

Why alcohol?
Oh! So foolish.
I need something
Says the drinker.

Why unwed sex?
Oh! So foolish?
Many partners
Lead to problems.

Why be so proud?
Oh! So foolish.
I am above
Anyone else.

What is money?
Oh! So foolish.
You want it fast
No matter what.

Why keep cussing?
Oh! So foolish,
Especially
Against others.

One without Jesus

One without Jesus,
You do not have life.
It is as simple
As I can say it.

Life with Jesus is
All I do ask for.
He makes me happy,
And He is so Good.

No hurry Jesus,
I will slow down now.
Spending time with
You is my desire.

I'm in love, Jesus,
With loving my Lord.
Obeying actions
To the Word of God.

Truth is in Jesus,
Salvation in Him.
Any other god
Will lead you to hell.

Praying to Jesus,
Thank, praise, and love.
It's not what I want
From God in getting.

Receiving Jesus
By stopping sinning.
God cannot look at
Unforgiven sins.

Knowing my Jesus
Does bring in the trust.
I do give my life
Totally to God.

Persecution

Life as a true Christian
Is being persecuted,
Some silent and some
Very noticeable.

I do believe that no
Actions that are so wrongful
Are the right things to do
For their many ideas.

Many say persecution
Does not happen in the
United States of America.
Not if you ignore hatred.

I do know God is Holy.
Many people do hate this,
Even in their own writings
And in their recruitment.

In the United States, we do
What are lawful in man's ways.
There are bad people who
Shall rule over others.

The Antichrist shall come
Into this world deceiving.
Many believe he'll do good
At first this is my thought too.

For now, I continue watching
The signs coming much closer
Together as in no other
Time in recorded history.

Radically Saved

People, do be a radical Christian today.
My prayers are to move Christians also.
Please live your life for our Lord Jesus.
Do truthfully know the True Way to God.

Are you hungry for the Word of God?
Do you want all times to read the Bible?
It is all about God's Special Creation.
Jesus had radically made a way for mankind.

We tell our loved ones all about Jesus
Since God had sent Jesus to die for us.
Do trust your lives with Jesus our Lord.
He is cleaning us and he is molding us.

Do not look for something new out there.
It is not in the name of your favorite star.
It is not in the music bands all around us.
It is only in the name of our dear Jesus.

We do reach out to unknown strangers.
We show them the Love Jesus gives us.
We go and help feed the homeless people.
We are interested as Christians for people.

We witness to other people around us.
The have so many lifestyles changes too.
They don't understand why there is no peace.
Now we as Christians will serve communities.

Holy Spirit is in the Holy Bible living in us
Many paths we do travel with His guidance.
The Savior Jesus is open to every sinner.
This is what makes a person whole today.

We pray for more souls to come to God.
The Great Commission tells us all to go.
We want to make disciples everywhere.
Come to the altar to speak to Jesus Christ.

We want to make a joyful noise unto Jesus.
We play the piano every chance we get.
Thank God for so many great hymns too.
Praise worship is one of my favorite times.

We do listen to God for answers today.
Our prayers to God are moving onward.
Almighty is the Jesus whom we do serve.
Always present with the Christian soldiers.

We do daily read the Word of God.
We try to understand by the Holy Spirit
Living within our heart to show us.
Do join the Christians reading our Bibles.

At justification, Christian get saved then.
Then at Baptism, we do understanding why.
In time, we will be wholly Sanctified too
When God give it to us if we do get it.

We will read the Living Word each day.
The Holy Spirit explains to us what we read.
The Holy Bible means what it really says
Do not think we can remove any of it

With Jesus's power, we can live sinless life.
The sins we did in the past is forgiven
When we truly give them to Lord Jesus.
We understand to release our sins to God.

We shall continue to study the Holy Bible,
For we know that Jesus really moves us.
Now we now know how underserving we
Were before we ever came to Jesus Christ.

We shall sing our songs before Lord Jesus,
For we are filled with Holy Spirit's Power.
Do lift up my soul with Christian music
So gracefully played by the musicians.

Rich Man of the Bible

Rich man of the Bible
Went away so sadly.
The price he had to pay
Was to give up riches.

Rich man of the Bible
Barns were torn on down
To build bigger barns now.
A fool who went to hell.

Rich man of the Bible
Remains in hell today.
His anguish and his pain
Lived without Jesus now.

We believed this man had
Gotten pleasures in life
Away from Lord Jesus,
Rejecting Holy God.

Is this one the same man?
He could have accepted
The living Grace of God,
Progressing to heaven.

If only he surrendered,
He could have helped the poor
With what he could have gave.
A different story.

From the Holy Bible,
What does these passages
Do mean in our own lives.
God said, "Come follow me."

Why does hell separate
Christians from lost people?
Lost people had never
Repented of their sins.

Saints

Saints are faithful
To the Church body.
We do reach out
To the perishing.

Saints are thankful
For God's abundance.
We give Jesus
Ourselves to His cause.

Saints are truthful
Handling the Bible.
We search for best
Interpretations.

Saints are open
To be true people.
We are never
To be in ourselves.

Saints are doing
More witnessing too.
We've gone out
To where the lost are.

Saints are praying
For God's own Power.
We speak to God
Wanting His Wisdom.

Saints are righteous Only in Jesus.
We show all lost the light of Jesus.

Saints are never
Above Lord Jesus.
We do obey
Whatever God says.

Satan Rages

Protect me from evil
When the devil rages.
God my deliverer
Take me and strengthen me.

I do write about God
Every chance I get.
Jesus Christ is my Lord
Whom gave me Inspiration.

Holy Spirit moves me.
Protection comes to me
Against wicked powers.
Greater is Jesus Christ.

The power of Satan
Uses people also.
His followers know him.
This Satan whom had lost.

Fallen angels cast out
Of heaven long ago.
Satan has nothing good
To say to Holy God.

Time is racing onward
To a final judgment.
Nothing Satan can do
To change God's only plan.

Father God, I believe
No matter what happens,
Life or death, I'm ready.
May Your Will be done God.

Seeker's Need Answers

God sees open lives;
Even lives we do hide.
We do sin today
Until we are hardened.

We do want freedom
In this world we live.
Many sin onward
Unconfessed to God.

Peace do eludes us.
It doesn't satisfy.
No one wants to die
And go on to hell.

Christians are happy
And do have something.
Should we go to God
In this wicked land?

The unsaved do talk
To a true Christian.
Do tell us what is
So important now.

What does Jesus do
That we can find peace.
We've done many things
We are ashamed of.

The Bible we do see
Is the hope we have.
Where should we start
To read more today?

Invited today
To Bible study.
We will go to it.
We do want to know.

Servant

A leader serves
Every day
To his people
They are given.

To serve takes our
Prayers and our thanks.
Even when tired,
We will obey.

There came a day
We turned away
Pride and power.
Now we serve.

God sent the needs
That we do see
As to help us
Grow in Jesus.

Greatest are they
Whom serves people.
Blessings are ours
Just to do this.

Holy Spirit
Moves my soul
To see God's
Own handiwork.

A miracle
That changes us.
We know it's God's
Healing power.

Master, we tell
Jesus our Lord
About loving
All the people.

God sees our faith
As a servant
To receive His
Power to serve.

Help the needy,
The sick and the
Poor nowadays.
God bless you.

Show God's servant
Appreciation.
Servant shows True
God's suffering.

Servant worships
Holy God too.
They are moving
With compassion.

God laid down all
To set us free.
Servant of God
Who does help all.

The cross of shame
Became God's plan
For all mankind.
He took our sins.

God's example
Shows us to be
Obedient.
Be more Christlike.

It is great love
To obey God
By doing His
Will in our lives.

Singing Songs, My God

Singing songs, my God
Knowing God loves me.
Father wanted all
To love Jesus back.

He sang the Psalms
On the Passover.
Jesus my Savior
Were in the Psalms.

The words of the Songs
Tells all about God.
His love speaks to me
How True Jesus is.

Songs melody does
Stays in my own mind.
It takes me onward
To sing unto God.

Chorus

True-to-life singing
We sing unto God.
Holy Father has
Sent Jesus His Son.

Sorry Downtown Ghetto

Sorry downtown ghetto,
We do feel for the people
Them whom need a hand up.
We Christians need to love.

Sorry downtown ghetto,
Money seems so scarce too.
It does seem so unfair.
Crimes seem to be upward.

Sorry downtown ghetto,
This place is so run-down.
People moving around
Alert to the dangers.

Sorry downtown ghetto,
Do we see past the fear?
Words can be uncaring
When we only go around.

Sorry downtown ghetto,
This part of town avoided.
Noise is all around too.
Crimes come to the many.

Sorry downtown ghetto,
Christians want to help too.
We do pray for ghetto
To do more than just talk.

Sorry downtown ghetto,
This land nobody wants.
Cannot build a business
On this bad location.

Sorry downtown ghetto,
Welfare is rampant here.
Must stay alive today.
Will children get the food?

Sorry downtown ghetto,
Jails are full of people
Whom come from the ghetto.
Violence does seem bad.

Sorry downtown ghetto,
I do have it better.
A nice neighborhood to
Keep it nice and clean too.

Sorry downtown ghetto,
The police sirens do
Seem a large part of life.
Do people want their help?

Sorry downtown ghetto,
Is seems so wicked too.
There are many people.
Can we drive down these roads?

Sorry downtown ghetto,
We think we've seen enough.
Life is not always fair.
How can we really help?

Sorry downtown ghetto,
Let the politicians help.
They may have solutions.
More Jesus many will say.

Sorry downtown ghetto,
Many voices, no solutions.
Riots may burn it down.
Hatreds seem so rampant.

Sorry downtown ghetto,
Life will just carry on.
Someday they tell you to
Leave so we can tear down.

Started Out Wrong

When I was a small boy,
I do remember hearing
About a man called Jesus,
Occasionally church.

Did I understand back then?
No, yet I heard good stories.
I do remember the teacher
Reading from the Holy Bible.

Sunday school consisted of
A desk to read about God.
Nowadays they have so much,
Yet at the time I did learn.

I finally got my Bible
With pictures in the Bible.
Had to say something good
To receive my Bible I wanted.

As time went onward then
I guess I had a choice.
I could stay home with my dad,
Or I could go to church with Mom.

I thought if it was important,
Why did nobody talk to me?
I thought was Jesus really God.
Was there anything to this?

When I did stay at home.
I did watch my dad cook
The Sunday meal back then.
It was my time with my dad.

I did feel good going to Church.
I stayed in the sanctuary.
Sunday School was an hour
Earlier Sunday morning then.

In my teens, I felt too old
To go to church back then.
I sometimes take songs
And changed the words then.

This would have been okay,
Yet sometimes I made fun
Of the Creator and of Jesus.
Even then I used to rhyme.

I knew the Bible was about
A God whom loved me so.
I still felt to go to church.
Many times I would dress up.

Eventually, I finished
The years of my high school.
I wondered why nobody
Mentioned they knew Jesus.

I guess it was the thing
Not to do when in high school
To mention what Jesus has done.
I was really a mess back then.

No more reason to stay at home.
A friend and I joined the navy.
I joined due to nothing better
To do with the time on my hands.

I never really did forget
How immature I was then.
Everything was either Yes sir
Or No sir to drill instructor.

Eventually out of boot camp
And out of radioman school,
I went on my first assignment
To the Island of Guam.

Testimony

In my life with no guidance from God,
I did whatever I thought was right to do.
There was a love or a hate in my actions.
No one, even myself, was ever satisfied.

God's standards were unknown to my living.
I did actions I thought I was right to do.
Little did I know then was I was fallen then.
Sin possessed me, and I did not see it then.

Morals were given, and I tried my best.
I thought being good was the way to go.
Everyone, especially I, had our excuses.
This rot was within my very own being.

The Bible I owned was important to me.
God was in this Bible that I held on to.
I knew somewhat Jesus was very important.
A man I had heard ruled all of mankind.

Somewhere along the way, I wanted to know.
If Jesus was God, is Jesus real to me or not?
I read the Bible without much understanding.
There was something special about Jesus.

Life moved onward, and I lived a sinful life.
I cannot say I was ever finding satisfaction.
It's like waking up from a hangover saying,
"I will never again drink beer or liquor again."

Sin continued to be a part of my wicked life.
I even went to church occasionally seeking.
At twenty-five, I read many Bible tracks.
This really began my journey towards God.

I asked God into my heart with a simple prayer.
I did not immediately understand the scripture.
I did grow slowly, and I did begin to mature.
Recently I was justified before a Holy God.

The Faithful

When we have Jesus
Moving in our lives,
Then the faithful ones
Will go with God's love.

Where are the faithful
Who are moved by grace?
They do live in all
The world nations.

Why has the world
Killed Christians so?
Satan moves the lost
Who do not know God.

Why do so many
Christians are to die?
They hated Jesus,
Martyrdom goes on.

Who knows the times, God,
When Jesus comes back?
Father God does know.
Holy Spirit shows.

Why Christian trials
We have in this life?
Let us be faithful
When He come for us.

Where do we find peace
In World turmoil?
Jesus our True God
Whom will give us peace.

When Jesus moves us
As faithful Christians,
He will keep with us
Wherever we go.

The Messiah

The Savior and the Master,
Jesus the Messiah
From the Holy Bible.

The Redeemer and the Life,
Jesus the Messiah
From the Holy Bible.

The Creator and the Vine,
Jesus the Messiah
From the Holy Bible.

The I Am and the Amen,
Jesus the Messiah
From the Holy Bible.

The Alpha and the Omega,
Jesus the Messiah
From the Holy Bible.

The Peace and the Love,
Jesus the Messiah
From the Holy Bible.

The Holy and the King,
Jesus the Messiah
From the Holy Bible.

The Righteous and the Word,
Jesus the Messiah
From the Holy Bible.

The Shepard and the Good,
Jesus the Messiah
From the Holy Bible.

The Mighty and the Just,
Jesus the Messiah
From the Holy Bible.

The Truth and the Word,
Jesus the Messiah
From the Holy Bible.

The Teacher and the Way,
Jesus the Messiah
From the Holy Bible.

Note: Only a few names of God

The Way, the Truth, and the Life

As we do pray,
The Word is the Way.
We talk to God
All alone then.

When we die too.
The Word is the Truth,
Jesus is Risen
From the sealed tomb.

Everlasting,
The Word is the Life.
He is alive
And there for you.

We do praise God,
The Word is Jesus.
We lift our hands
To feel His Love.

Lord Jesus Christ.
The Word is God.
Nobody but
Jesus forgives sins.

The Wonderful Mercy Jesus Gives Me

When I thought there was no hope,
Jesus came into my very own heart.
The wonderful mercy Jesus gives me.
He rescued me from fiery fires of hell.

So I began my journey towards my God.
Jesus leads me along the ways towards Him.
The wonderful mercy Jesus gives me.
He was with me everywhere I strayed to.

As I go each day with Jesus, I do pray.
He shows me to love Him along the way.
The wonderful mercy Jesus gives me.
He will stay with me in times of trouble.

Then I wonder am I really doing God's Will.
He knows I strive in prayers to obey Him.
The wonderful mercy Jesus gives me.
He will work with me and mold me right.

Should I forget to pray to my Holy Father,
He reminds me in His ways to keep talking.
The wonderful mercy Jesus gives me.
He does show me many times He loves me.

There I go not thinking before I begin talking.
He moves me to ask others for forgiveness.
The wonderful mercy Jesus gives me.
He tells me to be putting others first.

Now I believe Jesus will return very soon,
Jesus will come in a time without any warning.
The wonderful mercy Jesus gives me.
He knows my heart will be ready then.

Did I, God, do Your Will since my salvation.
He knows my desires on following Him.
The wonderful mercy Jesus gives me.
He knows my soul does thirst for Him.

Think about It

There is cleansing in the blood
Of the Lamb of God nowadays.
I shall trust in Savior Jesus
To make me clean before Father.

There is grace from Jesus Christ
Only way to our Holy Father.
I shall go to Lord Jesus
Accepting salvation by grace.

There is freedom from sinning
When Jesus was Resurrected.
I shall stop sinning Father
As I give my life to Jesus.

There is a hunger God
In my heart that wants Jesus.
I shall thirst for True Jesus
All the days of my own life.

There is a movement for Jesus
As Christians go out into world.
I shall obey Master Jesus
All the days of living for God.

There is only Faith in Jesus
That Christians do possess.
I shall put my faith in God
For God requires us to believe.

There is a trust in Jesus
To do what He says He'll do.
I shall trust Jesus in the
Life I'd given over to God.

There is wisdom in Jesus
As the Teacher and the Way.
I shall learn everything
I can from the Holy Bible.

Thoughts on Life

I'll be a slave today,
For God is my Master.
I will not go back
Thinking I can do it.

I know God's directions.
A relationship now.
Some say they know God' Will.
Many times, I get it right.

There are times I do sin.
Forgiveness is from God.
Sins are Satan's delight
Making Christians to fall.

My first Love is Jesus
I shall Love Him always.
The closer I get to
The Lord, I find His Truth.

What is the verdict now?
Can a person be just?
Do not sin onward now.
Yes, do think about God.

Satan does attack me.
Tough decision for some
Do use God's True Wisdom.
There are times I do fail.

Nothing is easy done
Earnestly obey God.
Why should I believe on this?
There is no easy life?

God is truly the Way.
He gave a choice back then.
The wide or narrow paths,
but which one do I choose.

Trinity

Our Father God, I AM.
First Person, Trinity.
He is Holy One, Almighty.
Maker of all, Eternity.

Our Son of God, I AM.
Second Person, Trinity.
Jesus bore sins, Crucify.
Christians saved, Messiah.

Our Holy Spirit, I AM.
Third person, Trinity.
Jesus gave us, Comforter.
Moves our souls, Redeemer.

Three are One, Trinity.
He is one God, Forever.
God loved mankind, forgiven.
We go to God, without sin.

Until the Trumpet Sounds

Until the trumpet sounds,
I shall be ready.
Up to my Jesus
I shall be going.

Right now until God comes,
I do continue
Up to my Jesus
I shall witness on.

I do praise Jesus
Every day too.
I know He's coming
To get me very soon.

No sleeping for me
Like the five virgins.
They missed Jesus Christ,
And they stayed here.

Victory is mine
The day Jesus comes.
He will see I stayed
Awake like the five virgins.

I'm saved by God's Grace;
Washed by Jesus's blood.
I will not work out
My own salvation.

The time comes swiftly
Before your eyes blink.
Christians will be gone.
Remaining are the lost.

Chaos will be
Worldwide event.
Who will be saved when
Jesus's Second Return comes?

Very Young and Very Lost

I grew up lost
A closed mind-set.
I do know I
Liked to have fun.

No one talked to
Me about God.
I did not know
The Gospel Stories.

I saw myself
Ready to do
Anything to
Pass time away.

I did not seek
Trouble back then
It always did
Come my own way.

Did not know why
I had to find
Life as a kid
Full of laughter.

I had dreams for
A need to be
Ready to see
Myself wishing.

Money I had
To find it by
Seeking it as
A need for pop.

Candy was to buy
With pop bottles
Along the road
Going on my bike.

I wasn't too bad
Within my acts
People thought I
Behaved myself.

Half the stories
Have not been told
By my writing
About events.

Now I'm older
Man looking back
As a Christian
I needed God.

This wide road in
Early childhood
Makes me wonder
Why I drifted.

God even had
A hand on me.
I believe this
To be the case.

Still I knew God
When I was small
Was up above.
Not, He is here.

We Cried "Amen"

The victory
In Lord Jesus,
We believed Him
We cried "Amen."

Prayers to God
In Jesus's name
Loving Him so
We cried "Amen."

Music to God
Beautifully
Sung from the heart
We cried "Amen."

Pastor read to
Congregation
From the Bible
We cried "Amen."

The sermon time
We encouraged
Pastor today
We cried "Amen."

Expound God's
Word in message
To be applied
We cried "Amen."

The altar call
For them who seeks
Prayers right now
We cried "Amen."

Their redemption
For salvation
God will answer
We cried "Amen."

What Good Things?

Saving my soul
Is God's Own Son.
I came to God
Repenting all.

Giving mercy
To this sinner
For the acts of
Transgressions.

Make me speak
Witnessing to
All in my path,
Give me boldness.

Listening God
My example
Is to be saved
Only by Grace.

I obey my God
By choosing Him.
Only in God
Is forgiveness.

True faith, I have
Holy Bible
To follow God,
Jesus, my faith.

Looking for Love
Came to be in
Jesus only.
No one else gives.

Spirit filled too.
Living in me
Is the person,
Holy Spirit.

Study God's Word
Is mine also.
I shall go on
This Narrow Way.

God's family
Is my brethren.
Thank you, Jesus
To be Christian.

I am a bride
And God is the
Bridegroom today.
I'm heaven bound.

In my free choice,
I went to God.
Satan lost me
He's a loser.

God, my visions
To only serve.
You bring insight
Into my life.

Wonderful God,
Mighty Jesus,
Holy Spirit
And He is One.

This searching man
Is looking now
To Jesus Christ.
I have New Life.

I choose never
To willful sin.
I look to God,
My example.

Wheat Fields

Over in the wheat fields did
Stand an old cross made of wood.
The sign on the cross did say,
"Jesus wants your own life too"?

Your life, Jesus does want it.
Are you totally committed?
Christians go out in the fields
And gather them for Jesus.

There is room for all by going
To lands that are far away.
Jesus had commanded us.
Let us obey Jesus Christ.

Let me tell others about God
Who needs Jesus desperately
To get their sins forgiven
By a God whom really cares.

Do Pastor the lost people
To trust all that Jesus says.
One thing the Bible says
Is to continue preaching.

Let the unsaved be saved now
Tell them the story of God.
Reveal to them the Father's
Plan for His Son Jesus Christ.

Why do Christians do delay
Sending out missionaries?
God shall supply your own needs
When you pray for Jesus's Will.

Jesus, forgive my failures
When I do feel defeated.
Holy Spirit builds me up
By going to the open fields.

Why Sin?

Jesus penetrates the darkest places.
We do go out, God, looking for the lost.
Hear us all people, youngest to oldest,
Hell reaches many who know not Jesus.

World missions, along with home missions,
Needs our prayers of the Christian churches.
Why go to them who knows nothing all
About love? Holy God is Holy Love.

God is not mushy sentimental love
Where people do say there is no judgment?
The Bible continues to be true now
The lost will be separated from God.

Will the people hear the true stories
From all past, now, and future living plans?
The only way to know the Written Word
Is by the Spirit revealing to us.

There are true Christians who do serve Jesus.
We love Jesus by following His Ways.
Father's love was Crucified, Calvary.
Holy Spirit now teaches on this Love.

We are trusting God to use us today.
Lost until we stop sinning willfully.
Our desires are Christian perfection
To where God cleanses us not to sin on.

Many say as Christians it is okay
To sin onward because we are human.
It is part of life we cannot change it
At justification, we stop sinning.

A person on our own can stop sinning.
Jesus, you're the one whom we do follow.
If you say we can live a sinless life,
We believe using Your strength and power.

Witnessing

Bible is placed out of sight
It will never trouble me.
This life is mine anyway.
I'm a winner in my sight.

I do ignore Christians now
They try to change my own ways.
Just what is a god anyway?
Atheist say there's no God.

A change is never easy
Why would I want to find out?
How else will life shall fail me?
Would Christian God help me now?

Life is to feel good also
Which god is the best lifestyle?
In my life, God's distant.
Can I gain the World out there?

Christian witnessing goes on
What is this they do tell me?
They may have something in life.
They seem very sure of themselves.

Just what is Holy Bible?
Holy Bible is God's Word.
It's thousand years old today.
No mistakes in the Bible.

Jesus died at Calvary
Hanging Cross had him on it.
Father's plan had Him to die.
The third day, Christ is alive.

Now I have heard the Gospel
It's finally making sense.
This I will surrender to.
Tell me how to do this now.

Wrong or True Actions

Our talk moves us
When we do see,
Yet we delay
To do the deed.

There's tomorrow
To witness too.
Spiritually,
It feels so good.

Father, hear us
Entertain too.
The music has
A dancing beat.

We do tell all
Of past works done.
We remember
What was done then.

After Sunday,
The less we pray.
We avoid all
Contact today.

Will people be
Including us?
We want the way
Of this world.

Accepted! Yes.
Rejection is
Not what we want.
Our light burns out.

I wish to be
Not forgotten.
Let me do this
Godless drinking.

Jesus's name is
Not a cuss word.
It is God's Son
They're talking too.

Blame society
Says the people.
Give us free gifts
To appease us.

Why do people
Fall into sin?
They say they were
Acting Christians.

We need Jesus
Immediately.
Our ways are not
The way to God.

The Bible sits
In stacks of books.
Our attitude
Is far from God.

Truest actions
Shows Jesus first.
Redeemed today
To sin no more.

Not a feeling,
We're required
To go to God
In faith and grace.

You cannot buy
What you do want.
Respect us we
Ask God today.

Lost to Saved

How do I feel, Jesus?
My vast sinfulness, God.
Your presence is not felt
Due to my own actions.

I had my desires
Jesus was not one of them.
Jesus wants me to come,
But my heart was so cold.

Independent, I was.
Unbelief made me lost.
I made my decisions
According to my needs.

My own wretchedness
Turned off lots of people,
Especially people
Who are not saved also.

Christians had prayed for me.
I was completely in
Satan's own domain now,
But God sent witnesses.

Holy Spirit opened
Myself to Jesus too.
I took my sins to God.
I prayed the sinner's prayer.

Lord, I feel accepted
Into the Christian body.
Now is the time to grow.
No staying as baby.

Forever, narrow road
To wonderful heaven.
I shall never return
To my own wretched days.

Precious Jesus

Oh! Precious Bible, Jesus
Reading it every day.
I do learn Jesus teachings
It is to keep me hungry.

Oh! Precious Living, Jesus
Whom does live on forever.
I do give Him my praises
It is holding on to God.

Oh! Precious Worship, Jesus
By encouraging Christians.
I do have a big thank-you
It is to keep listening.

Oh! Precious Loving, Jesus
Who does mold me forever.
I do love because I thirst
It is to love God today.

Oh! Precious Quiet, Jesus
Where I meditate on God.
I do be obedient
This is one way to Jesus.

Oh! Precious Prayers, Jesus
All through my daily living.
I do pray to Jesus Christ
It is to talk to my God.

Oh! Precious Music, Jesus
To know the hymns of my God.
I do sing to my Dear Lord
It is to keep me joyful.

Oh! Precious Teacher, Jesus
That has all my attention.
I do teach about Father
It's Holy Spirit guidance.

About the Author

Kevin Millage was in the Navy and Air Force for sixteen years and four months. He retired early from the Air Force. He has been writing poetry for thirty-four years but never published until now. He graduated from Andress High school in El Paso, Texas, in 1976. He took Bible courses through Hobe Sound Bible College of Hobe Sound, Florida, and edited several Bible courses. He is single and resides in Pennsylvania.

CPSIA information can be obtained
at www.ICGtesting.com
Printed in the USA
BVHW030757190719
553892BV00006B/15/P